TWENTYSOMETHING GIRL

TWENTYSOMETHING GIRL

1,001 QUICK TIPS AND TRICKS TO MAKE LIFE EASIER

By Melissa Fiorenza and Laura Serino
Illustrations By Kristina Hultkrantz

Arcade Publishing

Arcade Publishing books may be purchased in bulk at special
discounts for sales promotion, corporate gifts, fund-raising, or
educational purposes. Special editions can also be created to
specifications. For details, contact the Special Sales Department,
Arcade Publishing, 307 West 36th Street, 11th Floor, New York,
NY 10018 or info@skyhorsepublishing.com.

Arcade Publishing® is a registered trademark of Skyhorse
Publishing, Inc. ®, a Delaware corporation.

Visit our website at www.arcadepub.com

10 9 8 7 6 5 4 3 2 1

Library of Congress Cataloging-in-Publication Data is available
on file.

ISBN: 978-1-61145-763-6

Printed in China

CONTENTS

INTRODUCTION

If you're a twentysomething girl, chances are you have friends that are married, engaged, single, full-time mothers, and total workaholics. You might own a house, have a healthy 401k and zero debt, but be best pals with a gal that lives month-to-month and is riddled with student loan and credit card bills. If you're in grad school, your best friend might already be a vice president at a company. Suffice it to say, we're all on different paths. It's what makes our generation so complex. We were the first to grow up with the Internet (and learned patience when connecting to AOL) and now we can't walk anywhere without our smart phones. We were part of the "self-esteem" generation where we were told that we can do anything and everything, but as we've gotten older, we've realized just how hard that's going to be. On top of our towering expectations, we're inundated with promises on how to make our chaotic lives a hell of a lot easier: how to lose five pounds in five days, get the job you want in ten steps, one hundred ways to give him an orgasm.

With suggestions, tutorials, and do-this, do-that tomes of never-ending guidance that come in the form of Google, magazines, e-books, apps, podcasts, smoke signals, and hieroglyphics, (you name it, it's out there), the onslaught of information can become a little dizzying. Our lives are incredibly busy and it'd be nice if there were less search engines and more reliable help out there, right? Wouldn't it be great if there was a book that waded through all the clutter and just delivered the good stuff you need to know to make this crazy decade . . . easier? We realized such a book was missing: a guide that streamlines all the helpful advice out there into bite-sized tips to help make life just a little bit easier in all different categories. We give you *Twentysomething Girl*.

We first met when we worked together back in 2006 in New York City at *Quick & Simple* magazine, a weekly off-shoot of *Good Housekeeping*. Its taglines were along the lines of "all tips, all the time," and "buy it weekly, use it daily." In other words, it was all about fast, easy tips—ones you could read in a split second and use for the rest of your lives. We became borderline obsessed with great advice that we could pass on to others. After *Q&S*, Laura went on to *Family Circle* magazine and Melissa to *All You*—where quick tips were once again the norm—then on from there to write for a broad range of publications, websites, and companies. Even after we hung up our editor heels for a slower paced life, we still kept our penchant for the give-it-to-me-straight kind of wisdom.

Here's how we propose you read *Twentysomething Girl*: Grab a cup of tea, coffee, or wine and start on page one. Even if you're not looking for advice on money or career right now, just read it. The one thing you can't really Google is a tip you're not yet looking for. With this book, we promise you'll find tips you may have never sought out, but you'll be glad you did. Plus, we deliver it in the way we've promised you we love: quick, easy, and straight to the point. You can read it standing up on the subway or in a crowded

Starbucks and not miss a beat, because the best advice for a modern, on-the-go girl is dispensed quickly. Once you've read it all the way through, keep it on your bookshelf and return to it when you can't remember that one tip, when you need an idea for a house party, or when you want to find out how to clean up red wine without reading a million suggestions for the best result.

We're not here to teach you, we're here to help. We've spent the past decade of our twenties writing down the stuff we learned, the stuff that stayed with us, and the mistakes we already made so you don't have to. And that, friends, is not something you can find in a search engine.

Lots of luck to you,
Melissa & Laura

BEAUTY

"YOU DON'T KNOW HOW HARD IT IS BEING
A WOMAN LOOKING THE WAY I DO."

—*Jessica Rabbit*

It's time to put our best face forward. Whether that means finding the perfect shade of lipstick or applying sunblock every morning, taking care of our bodies from head to toe isn't just a vain endeavor—it's the right thing to do. There's a good reason why it's perfectly acceptable to treat yourself to a smart beauty routine: looking good on the outside boosts your confidence on the inside. Without going into all the trends you read in your favorite beauty mags, here are our timeless beauty basics that'll give you that top-to-bottom glow from the inside out.

PRETTY LITTLE MAKEUP TIPS

When your eyeliner pencil tip starts to get crumbly, toss it in the freezer. After ten minutes, it should be firm enough to use on your skin.

Blow-dry your eyelash curler for ten seconds before using it for a more effective curl.

Bummed about your lipstick choice? Don't assume the store won't take it back. Places like CVS and even some big department stores will actually offer a full refund for opened and even partially used products.

Before applying eye shadow, dab a little foundation or powder on your lids. It will help keep shadow on for longer.

Your makeup brushes need a bath, too. Try to do it at least every two weeks; just use a drop of baby shampoo and rinse with warm water, then reshape the bristles and let them airdry.

Washing dishes barehanded helps weaken nails, so always slip on rubber gloves first.

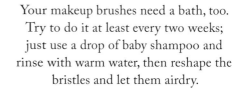

A 2011 study led by a Harvard Medical School assistant professor showed that women who wear makeup are seen as more competent. Even if you're not trying to impress anyone at the office or in class, dab on a little blush and mascara for good measure.

Out of makeup remover and sporting waterproof mascara? Olive oil + cotton ball = instant removal.

"BEAUTY, TO ME, IS ABOUT BEING COMFORTABLE IN YOUR OWN SKIN. THAT, OR A KICK-ASS RED LIPSTICK."
—GWYNETH PALTROW

Love, love, love trying new beauty products? Your wallet doesn't share the same hobby. Lucky for you, there's Birchbox.com: Pay ten bucks a month to have beauty samples delivered to your door throughout the year, complete with explanations and how-tos.

For a balanced, natural look, jazz up either your eyes or your lips—never both for daytime. A heavier look is usually best reserved for evenings.

A beige eye pencil in the corner of your eyes and a bright cheek color for your face is the secret to an "I'm not hungover and ridiculously tired" look.

Real Chick Tip

Dust baby powder on your eyelashes before you apply your mascara. It will help make your lashes look fuller and longer.

−Jessica, 23, MA,
graphic designer

YOUR TRUE COLORS

It's the age old question that, for some reason, we always forget the answer to: What should I wear to make my peepers pop? Alayne Curtiss, celebrity makeup artist and owner of Make Me Fabulous in Ballston Spa, New York, made it easy for us to remember: *contrast, baby*. Here's what she taught us …

THE COLOR WHEEL RULE

If you look at a color wheel, the color opposite your eye color will make your own eye color pop. So if you have green eyes, wearing green eye shadow may be fighting your own eye color. If you have…

BLUE EYES

Try warm copper tones and peaches

GREEN EYES

Try pinks and violets

BROWN EYES

This is really a combination of many colors, so you can try lots. If you have gold or green flecks in your brown eyes, try blues and violets.

HAZEL EYES

Try a variety of shades and see what happens! If you want your eyes to look greener, use pinks and violets. If you want your eyes to look bluer, try copper and peaches. If you want your eyes to look browner, try blues and violets.

ANY COLOR EYE

Alayne's favorite eye tone that brightens almost any eye and looks great on most skin tones is a soft peach tone swept over the lid. She also recommends putting a nude or skin colored peach tone along the inner rim of tired eyes, of any color, to mask the redness when feeling overly tired.

Her picks: Bare Escentuals Vanilla Sugar Eye Shadow and Glo Minerals Peach Pencil.

Truth is: You don't have to use foundation, no matter what every "five things you must wear daily" article says. Opt for a BB cream or a tinted moisturizer for barely-there coverage, or if your skin is naturally perfect (ya jerk), skip it.

Use a little mascara before applying false lashes to help them stay in place.

Gloss is better than lipstick when you're trying to achieve fuller-looking lips.

Wherever you're shopping for beauty products, ask about free samples, sales, coupons, and deals. Beauty salespeople recognize that their products are luxuries, not necessities, and will often be willing to help you afford them.

There's nothing like hitting the spa with your girls for a pampering sesh, but that stuff adds up. Next time, pony up for just a pedicure: it lasts much longer than a mani and then you can catch up on the latest gossip rags at the same time.

If you're applying lip balm with your fingers, rub the excess goo on your nail cuticles—moisturizing multitasking!

HAIR CARE—THE MANE EVENT

Treat your hair to a quick burst of cold water right before you finish your shower—it helps flatten and seal the cuticles to give you shine.

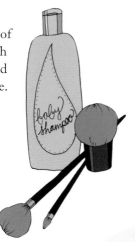

If you're one of those *did-I-turn-off-my-flat-iron* kinda girls, always say out loud: "Today is [day here], and I turned it off" as soon as you turn it off. When you're in the car wondering if you did, you'll remember saying it.

Shampoo every two days. Doing it daily can dry out your hair. If your hair tends to look oily without a daily wash, try dry shampoo at the roots.

Three words: boar bristle brush.

The high setting on your dryer may actually be too hot for your hair—which can cause damage. That said, towel dry a little first and go about your normal routine, then use the dryer.

Although the shampoo bottle says to use it with the corresponding conditioner, news flash: You don't need to. In fact, feel free to mix and match: a volumizing shampoo with a color protecting conditioner is a-okay.

Dancing with the idea of bangs? Hit up a wig shop to test out the look. (Also try it if you're thinking of going platinum blonde or Rihanna red, too). Or try on a hairstyle at thehairstyler.com.

No time for a full blow-out? Just dry your part line and the frame of your face before you rush out.

Spot a teeny, tiny gray hair—and you're only 24? Don't fret, pet, it happens. Swipe it with mascara and get on with your day.

When you have a specific style or updo in mind, hit up Pinterest or the Interwebs and drag all relevant photos to your desktop. Combine in a one-page Word doc and slap it on your hair stylist's console. Most of them will agree: A picture is worth a thousand verbal descriptions.

Got flyaways and no product to deal with them? A swipe of clear mascara or a dryer sheet should do the trick.

For a quick volume boost without hopping in the shower, bend over and spritz dry shampoo on your roots. A root lifter works well, too.

Hair stylists massage your head in the sink for a reason—it stimulates your scalp, which is vital for awesome hair. So when at home, don't just toss on shampoo and rinse—give your fingertips a workout and rub your roots.

Real Chick Tip

Unfortunately, an unlimited hair budget is not an option for me. I stick to my regular trusted salon for super permanent changes like coloring and major cuts— but for trims and washes, I frequent the far less expensive chains in the area. They get the same job done for less than half the price.

–Emily, 23, NY,
social media manager

WAXING POETIC

Say sayonara to unwanted hair with a wax appointment, stat. Already do that? Jessica Coba, European Wax Center Co-Founder and Chief Executive Officer gave us the hairy details on how to achieve the perfect wax:

1. **Exfoliate first.** It's important to exfoliate your skin with gentle solutions. Removing dead skin cells before getting hair removed will reduce the chance of ingrown hairs, bumps, and blemishes, which is great, especially near the bikini area.

2. **Wax first, spray tan later.** Waxing opens your pores so be sure to keep your skin free of dirt, oil and other pore-clogging solutions. Wait at least 48 hours before hitting the spray tan booth or heading to the gym to avoid ingrown hairs, bumps, and blemishes.

3. **Hydrate, hydrate, hydrate!** After ridding yourself of body hair, drink lots of water and use film-free lotions that will help lock in moisture. This will leave your skin glowing year-round.

4. **Drop that razor.** You never want to shave any part of your face. Once you shave your face or any other area, the hair will grow back coarser and appear darker. Waxing is the best way to keep your facial hair light, soft, and less noticeable for much longer.

5. **Time it right.** You could be more sensitive in the bikini area when waxing during your menstrual cycle. However, waxing other areas such as your eyebrows, underarms, or legs most likely will not be more sensitive. If you decide to wax at that time and you feel more sensitive, simply let your Wax Specialist know and reschedule for when you are feeling better. The pain tolerance will really depend on each person and how they are feeling.

STRIKE A POSE!
HERE'S HOW TO ROCK . . .

FULL-LENGTH SNAPSHOTS . . .
Stand up straight and do *not* let your arms hang limp by your side. Put a hand on your hip or both in your back pockets, anything to get them un-lifeless.

YOUR LINKEDIN PICS . . .
Just use a headshot, where your hair is done and your makeup is nice and natural. And wear something that shows that you're, uh, wearing something. No strapless tops or tank tops.

YOUR FACEBOOK PIC . . .
Don't look drunk and don't look full of yourself. Choose a pic that represents you—you curling up with your pup, fishing with your pops, or casually smiling next to a friend are all smart options that won't come across as obnoxious.

ALL PHOTOS . . .
Suck in, shoulders back, and position yourself at eye level with the lens or slightly above (no double chins here). Then put yourself at ease: Close your eyes, then open them right before the camera is clicked. Push your tongue against your top teeth to get the perfect smile.

LOVE YOUR SKIN

To nix dark circles under your eyes—a pretty sensitive area on your face—invest in a vitamin-laden concealer that is a shade lighter than the foundation you use.

Ever get little white raised bumps around your eyes, that aren't necessarily pimple-like? They may be skin tags, which are harmless. Ask your derm or facial lady if they can remove them for you.

 Always remove makeup before you hit the hay. Most makeup remover wipes are made of the same ingredients, so don't blow your budget on pretty packaging.

Got chapped or cracked lips, like, all the time? Apply Aquaphor by Eucerin ointment to your puckers before bed. We swear by it.

Great time to moisturize your dry, dry skin: Right after you take a shower. Slather on that lotion like it's your job.

If you hit the gym during your lunch hour and don't want to return to your 2 p.m. meeting looking flushed, wrap a cold, wet towel around your neck to help lower your body temp and reduce the redness.

FACE IT—YOU NEED THESE TIPS

We asked Shiri Sarfati, skin care expert and executive vice president of Repêchage, to give us her best advice when it comes to all things healthy skin. Here goes:

YOUR DAILY ROUTINE

Cleanse your skin twice daily in three steps: cleansing, exfoliating, and toning. It should take between seven and ten minutes; although it sounds like a lifetime, your skin will thank you well into your thirties!

- To cleanse: look for a cream or gel cleanser that is soap-free, as soap dehydrates the skin. Massage into your skin and remove with clean cotton.

- To exfoliate: Apply a granular exfoliating mask, and leave on for five minutes. The granular particles will help physically lift out debris and impurities from the skin. Remove with cotton rather than a washcloth to prevent bacteria or detergents from further irritating the skin.

- To tone: Spray on a toner to flush out the pores and rebalance the pH of the skin.

HOW TO POP THAT PIMPLE

As tempting as that whitehead may look, refrain from squeezing with your fingertips. Bacteria from under your nails may cause infection, or worse, you may end up scarring your skin. Instead, visit a skin care professional to properly remove bumps. You can also dab a solution with salicylic acid, kojic acid, and sulfur on to your skin to melt away your blemish overnight . . . If you *must* pick, wrap both index fingers in facial tissue, pull skin apart finding the source of the clogged plug and then gently lift out. Don't push down on your skin as this will cause further irritation.

Next time you wake up with a Venn diagram on your face, thanks to your pillow smushed up against your skin, a few splashes of warm water should nix the creases fast. (Is your pillow a repeat offender? Go buy a satin or silk pillowcase.)

Fragrance travels upward, so spritz perfume behind your knees in addition to the nape of your neck.

Your neck ages fast. Keep it looking young by not forgetting it when you're putting on sunscreen or your daily moisturizer.

Prone to puffy eyes? Using two pillows when you sleep, and hence elevating your head, will drop those suckers fast.

Cover up lotion-soaked feet with Saran wrap, then cozy socks and sleep in that for a night = sexy, smooth soles. Rough calluses, be gone.

Reason #4,987 to get your Zs: your complexion goes to work, repairing damage that was done the day before.

Forget super, duper expensive facial scrubs. Use a little sugar as you wash your face.

Buy a humidifier to use during the winter time. If you have a roomie, tell them you need it for skin purposes. Keeping your room properly moisturized does wonders for your skin.

NAIL YOUR NEXT MANI

Who better to give quick nail tips than nail guru Deborah Lippmann? She suggests getting a weekly manicure at home or at the salon. If seeing a weekly manicurist isn't in the budget, here's how you can get a proper manicure *chez vous*.

1. **Hydrate.** Moisturize your hands and cuticles after every time you wash your hands. Your nails will begin to look better instantly.

2. **Cleanse.** Use polish remover on a piece of cotton, press onto each nail for five seconds and remove.

3. **Shape.** File from each outside edge toward the center of the nail. Try your best to make each nail length the same. Push back your cuticles with a cuticle pusher and nip any remaining skin. Apply oil and massage it in.

4. **Choose your base coat.** Find the right treatment based on the state of your nails. Go for a rehydrating one for brittle nails or ridge filler if nails are uneven. (We love Deborah's Hard Rock formula as a base *and* top coat.)

5. **Apply color.** Remove brush from the bottle by pulling it back along the neck of the bottle. Start at the center of the nail and nudge the brush toward the cuticle and then towards the tip of your nail. Repeat on either side until nail is covered with lacquer. Let dry a minute and apply a second coat.

6. **Finish.** A top coat will keep your polish lasting well until your next at home mani.

CAREERS

"NEARLY EVERY GLAMOROUS, WEALTHY, SUCCESSFUL CAREER WOMAN YOU MIGHT ENVY STARTED OUT AS SOME KIND OF SCHLEP."

—*Helen Gurley Brown*

Congratulations, you've graduated college!
Or maybe that was three years ago and you still don't know
what you want to be when you grow up. Navigating a career
can be tricky. One thing you must remember—any job is
within your grasp. We're at an age where it's perfectly
acceptable to switch job fields, take an internship, or go for
a gig just because it pays well. Whatever you think your next
career step is, we've got easy tips that will take you from the
waiting room to a front office in no time at all.

ON APPLYING FOR JOBS

Set up a mock interview with three different people. Take it seriously. Figure out which questions get you stumped so you can think ahead.

No matter what industry you're in, have a suit ready to go in your closet . . . just in case.

Work your contacts. If a friend of a friend knows someone at a company you're applying to, send them a casual email. Be brief: explain how you got their email and attach your resumé. The rest is up to fate.

Use the job posting as a guide while writing your cover letter and tweaking your resumé. If you're applying for a product management position, make sure the words "product" and "management" fall somewhere in there. Match up keywords, address the skills they're looking for, and put your most relevant accomplishments on top.

Always try to quantify your success stories on your resumé. Here's what we mean: "Increased revenue by 60%," "Managed 30 venues," or "Raised $20,000 for . . ."

Get your resumé and cover letter professionally edited. Monster.com offers the service starting at $140. Or pass it along to a friend who has a knack for the written word.

A growing trend in certain industries is personal websites. If you have clips, photos, public cases, or something visual that you could collect on a site, along with your resumé, consider building your own page and referencing it on your resumé for potential employers to visit. Weebly.com is a good place to start.

If you're interested in a company that isn't hiring, set up an informational interview, requesting to meet and ask questions about the company. If a spot does open up down the line, your name will stand out among the applications.

Send out your resumé in a universal PDF format. With all the different computers, programs, and computer-challenged people out there, you don't want to send a resumé that your interviewer can't open.

Keep your contacts in one place, like LinkedIn.com. Or hey, stick them all in a little black book.

"I GET MAD AT PEOPLE WHO TALK ABOUT TRAUMATIC JOB INTERVIEWS, ABOUT GOING ON ONE AND GETTING REJECTED. I GET RE-JECTED ALL THE TIME AND NOT ONLY DO I GET REJECTED, BUT PEOPLE HAVE NO PROB-LEM BEING REALLY SPECIFIC ABOUT WHY I WAS REJECTED."
—JULIA SWEENEY

Network! And then don't stop networking. Join organizations and volunteer groups, attend events and industry conferences, and get on your college alumni's database. You never know who could be the key ingredient to helping you land a job.

Applying for a sought-after position can be intimidating, but don't be afraid to find out where your resumé stands. Follow up after a week. Not everyone will be able to respond to every applicant, but a quick email can reiterate your desire for the position. Don't follow up more than once though— nobody wants to hire the desperate girl.

Keep in touch with everyone you've had a good working relationship with. After you leave a job or internship, email your former supervisor to say hello and to update them on your life. It will help down the line when you are asked to give references.

Spiff up your resumé. Don't be afraid to give it a little personality, like a monogram or a list of hobbies that are relevant to the job you're seeking.

JOB SITES WORTH YOUR TIME

Bookmark these bad boys when you're cruising for openings.

- simplyhired.com
- monster.com
- hotjobs.yahoo.com
- indeed.com
- linkedin.com
- craigslist.org

- careerbuilder.com
- glassdoor.com
- dice.com
- mediabistro.com
- tweetmyjobs.com
- snagajob.com

Intern, volunteer, do something to get your foot in the door! If a company you'd love to work for is searching for "unpaid interns," sometimes it can help to suck it up and do it, even if it's only for one day a week.

Immediately after ending an internship, write a thank-you note to your supervisor and team letting them know you appreciate the opportunity and learned a lot. Include your contact information so you can keep in touch.

When you're applying to a job online, take the extra few minutes to hunt down the name of the HR recruiter and put his/her name in your cover letter, instead of writing: "To Sir or Madam."

Accept business cards like you've just been handed the answer to a million dollar question. Look it over for a few seconds before you tuck it away.

Research the company you're interviewing with. Know their mission statement and know who runs the company.

When you're asked to put down salary requirements, do keep your previous pay scales in mind. But you should also check out a salary calculator online to see what range of money is usually given for the position you're going for.

THE ALL-MIGHTY INTERVIEW

Avoid negative comments about past employers or coworkers during all interviews. You don't want to look like you can't easily get along with anyone.

Don't send your references in until you're asked for them. When asked for references, ask how many they'd prefer to contact.

Jot down a list of accomplishments and achievements you want to remember to bring up during the course of conversation. Read it every night for a week before the big day, so you don't forget to mention one.

Always have questions prepared for the end of the interview to show that you did your research and really are interested in the position. A great go-to opener: "What's your favorite part about working here?" But after that, avoid asking more broad questions. Poke around on the company website and think of a smart question to ask them ahead of time. Let them know you've done your research.

Fifteen minutes early is out, five minutes is in. Get there just before the interview, so your interviewer doesn't feel like they have to greet you immediately.

Lighten up. You want to be formal in an interview, but don't be afraid to crack a joke or poke fun at yourself if a good situation arises. People will want to work with you if you're fun to be around.

Shower the receptionist with kindness. She sees all, knows all, and reports often about the candidates that walk through that front door and have a seat.

Always bring at least three extra resumés with you to an interview. Wow them even more with a resumé, a sample portfolio, and references in a folder. Nothing says, "I'm ready to be hired" more than being prepared for a background check.

Send a thank you note via snail mail and email. Emails get lost, but snail mail takes a couple days. Hedge your bets and do both. Drop in a line from the meeting that will make them remember you (i.e. Hope your poodle Fifi is feeling better!).

When you're interviewing for a job, learn all you can about how you can grow in the position you're after—are promotions regular? Or will you be stuck in the same spot for years to come?

Real Chick Tip

After working on four magazines simultaneously at one company, they asked me to take on a fifth. Not only was I overworked, but this additional publication required lots of extra attention and experience that I simply didn't have. When I voiced my concerns to supervisors, they suggested I get help with organization and prepare for this growing experience for myself. I suggested they pay me more but my opinions fell on deaf ears. Shortly afterward, I notified my boss that it would be my last day. I learned that it's important to recognize that sometimes you're put into situations that aren't ideal and you feel trapped. When that happens, you have to stand up for yourself. Never settle, never sell yourself short, and never look back.

−Karina, 26, NY, photo editor

TELL ME ABOUT YOURSELF . . .

Before you head out to the all-important job interview, cram with these popular interview questions. Know the answers inside and out, practice with a friend, a mirror, a pet, a stiletto—anything. Just know them.

- What brings you here today?
- What are your greatest weaknesses?
- How would your best friend, or previous coworkers, describe you?
- What are your long- and short-term goals?
- Describe an obstacle you overcame in the past year.
- Why do you want to work here?
- What are your greatest strengths?
- What have you done to expand on your experience?
- Tell me about a time when you failed.
- Tell me about a time when you succeeded.

Sources: careerbuilder.com; monster.com; wisebread.com

EMPLOYERS ARE ALL A-TWITTER!
Do you tweet? You should—if only for the special discounts companies dish out *and* the growing number of jobs listed. Follow the hashtag #Tweetmyjobs to see an always-updating stream of open positions.

DRESS TO IMPRESS

Be it for a corporate setting or business casual, here's a sure-fire outfit that every smartly dressed gal should wear to an interview. (Ladies applying for a fashion-related gig: throw the rules out the window.)

- A white button-down or blouse. Make sure it fits well and has no yellowing stains. Pair it with a pencil skirt or perfectly tailored pants.
- Add a shot of color with a cardigan or bright necklace.
- Wear a pump. It shows you're mature. Just make sure the heel is less than three inches so you don't look too overdressed.
- Carry a smart bag—think leather or canvas tote (nothing studded or glittery).

CONGRATS! YOU'RE HIRED. NOW WHAT?

When you're starting a new job, be friendly to everyone—regardless of who you hear is the office villain. You don't want to make enemies from the get go.

When you snag the ever-so-special job offer, don't forget: get it in writing, ask for time to think it over (if you need it), and negotiate anything from your salary to vacation days.

Avoid office gossip. Every office has a know-it-all and trust us, you don't want to be it. It's called a workplace for a reason, so keep that in mind when your cube buddy wants to discuss whom your boss was seen out with over the weekend.

Messed up at work? Fess up, apologize to your supervisor, and let it go. You can only do more harm by continuing to bring it up and apologizing profusely. They get it, you're sorry. Everyone makes mistakes.

Don't steal office supplies. Does this really need to be said?

Avoid using your computer and workstation for personal use. Sure, it's okay to check your Facebook page during lunch, but there's no need to download photos from the weekend to your desktop.

If your workplace offers educational classes, volunteer opportunities, or a lunch buddy program, do it up. The right work environment will help you to grow as a person if you cash in on opportunities.

Ask new coworkers about the best places to grab breakfast, lunch, or coffee; it's a great way to get into a conversation and may lead to a lunch invitation. Bonus: New friends!

You're going to come across someone who is jealous, insecure, mean, or difficult to work with. You'll definitely be the punching bag for someone at some point. Fingers will be pointed at you. Never point them back. Don't sink to their level. Maintain a good attitude with everyone around you. Don't bitch about work at work. Save it for happy hour with your girlfriends.

Don't be a slob. Keep your desk area clean. If you've got clutter, shove it in a drawer.

Stash a toothbrush, gum, or mints in your desk drawer at all times. If you're called into a one-on-one meeting, you won't have to worry that your nasty breath is permeating the room.

A quick, easy way to meet people: leave a bowl of candy on your desk.

Know everyone's names. Your desk mate. The boss that doesn't talk to you. The janitor. You should be invested in the people around you.

Stay hidden online. Keep your blog, Facebook, and Twitter accounts separate from work, and for the love of God, never post anything bad about your company online—not even about how revolting taco day is in the cafeteria.

Ever head to the conference room for a meeting and have to sit there for fifteen minutes because the attendees are running late? Bring some work with you that you can do while waiting. It'll not only show others your fabulous productivity skills, but that's one less thing you'll have to do when you get back to your desk.

Never bring a leftover fish dinner to work. And if you do, don't microwave it in the communal kitchen. Just trust us on this one.

Do we need to say it again? Do not Facebook, IM, tweet, or post anything about how bad your day at work is going. You'll eventually get caught and reprimanded. Keep it to yourself or vent to someone after hours.

Be conscious of smells in general. Don't stroll in with gallons of perfume on. It's not as bad as bringing in fish but hey, you'll still stink.

If you have a master plan or a great idea, it goes to waste if you keep it to yourself. Start from the ground up and pitch it to your direct supervisor first.

It's easy to lose motivation when you're sitting in a cubicle. Jazz it up with fake or real flowers, pictures (nothing incriminating; skip the one of you and the girls on spring break downing tequila), magazine covers that sparked your eye, newspaper headlines you want to keep forever, and colorful portraits or trinkets.

Even if your coworker has a sailor's mouth on her—and your superiors never seem to care when she drops the F-bomb—don't take that as an OK for you to go ahead and curse, too. Even though no one says anything, they may find it really unprofessional.

Wear shoes to work that you can walk in. If you get called to a last minute meeting and you walk in like a horse in heat because your platforms aren't broken-in, you'll look more like an undergrad than a colleague.

Does everyone eat lunch at his or her desk? Do people arrive before 9am? Understand the social cues. Can't seem to find a common thread? Lucky you! It's a free-for-all!

Whenever you're presented with a good chance to do so, praise a coworker in front of everyone. It's completely flattering to the person you're complimenting, and they'll remember that you did that. It also shows good teamwork, like you know that the job doesn't rely on just you.

The median annual earnings of women fifteen or older who worked full-time all year in 2008 was $35,745. It was actually higher the year before, at $36,451. Come on, ladies, if you think you deserve a raise, ask for one—but be ready to cite specific reasons for why you should get it.

Brown bag it at least twice a week. You'll save money and eat healthier. Plus it will force you to use your kitchen.

When someone compliments you on your work, don't respond with anything negative like, "Oh, it was nothing," or "It wasn't that awesome." Just say thanks.

Speed up productivity—and look really cool—by speeding up your typing. Take a few tests and learn how to double your time at typingtest.com. It even shows you how much time you'll save per week by getting better.

"EVERYONE HAS AN INVISIBLE SIGN HANGING FROM THEIR NECK SAYING, 'MAKE ME FEEL IMPORTANT.' NEVER FORGET THIS MESSAGE WHEN WORKING WITH PEOPLE."
—MARY KAY ASH

Don't flirt with coworkers, at least not during office hours. It's common to meet people at work that you'll want to date. Invite them to happy hour and chat it up there—just don't use the copy room as a meet-up spot for your sexy trysts.

Take notes in meetings. Even if it's a quick briefing, have a pad of paper and pen on you at all times to show that you're paying attention and absorbing the information you're given.

Don't keep shoes in a desk drawer. It will start to smell and then you'll be the stinky shoe girl at work.

If you work for a law firm, subscribe to policy journals. A marketing firm? Read *Ad Age*. Keep informed and up-to-date in your area of expertise in order to remain relevant and be able to have engaged conversations with coworkers.

If you're having trouble working with someone, sit down and try to hash it out. At the core, you're both just people at work with your own stuff going on at home. It's better to politely and directly ask someone what it is you're doing wrong than be passive aggressive about it.

Personal grooming belongs at home. If you need to brush your teeth, floss, or touch up makeup, head to the ladies room. Never tweeze your eyebrows or clip your nails at your desk.

Even if your performance review rocks, ask if there are any areas you can improve on in the future.

Got a glowing email from the boss? Congrats! Now save it forever. In fact, print it and keep it at home. You can use these in the future to remind yourself of specific achievements when prepping for an interview, or even just for quick mood boost.

Real Chick Tip

Know everyone. When I was an undergrad, I worked three semesters as a production assistant for CBS. My director more or less assured me he would create a position for me after graduation. The week I finished school, he left the company. I thought I was screwed. Thankfully in my time there, he thought so highly of me that he introduced me to several other important people in different divisions of the company, one of whom I ultimately reached out to—and who gave me my first big girl job.

–Andrea, 27, NYC,
Columbia University grad student

Remember the power of "I" statements. If your boss never told you about a looming deadline, never say "You never told me that." Instead, say "I must have forgot to mark it in my calendar. Can we take five minutes to rehash it so I can get it done pronto?"

Avoid saying anything negative about someone's idea or project in an email; those things are so easily forwarded or accidentally printed, you could become the office beotch in a matter of seconds.

Out with a group? Don't be the first one to order an alcoholic beverage, and please, please limit yourself. You're a classy lady—remember that.

Keep your cool. If you're angry, upset, or frustrated, don't let it show. You're a mature woman in the workplace and you should act like a lady no matter what.

"EARNING HAPPINESS MEANS DOING GOOD AND WORKING, NOT SPECULATING AND BEING LAZY. LAZINESS MAY LOOK INVITING, BUT ONLY WORK GIVES YOU TRUE SATISFACTION."
—ANNE FRANK

When you want to say hi to a colleague or client outside the office, but are afraid they won't remember your name, take the pressure off. Intro yourself like this: "Jeff Haskell? Kate Smith . . . nice seeing you again!"

Delegate, delegate, delegate. You may think it looks good to take a lot on your plate and handle it all yourself, but not always.

Save the personal calls for your lunch hour. *Outside*. On your *cell phone*. No one wants to hear you complain to your Mom about your sister's upcoming nuptials.

Walk away from your computer and touch your toes, do a head roll, or just do a loop around the office every hour to give your eyes a rest and your body a jolt.

Vacation should be about sipping strawberry daiquiris on a beach in Montego Bay, pondering: jerk chicken or shrimp? Nowhere in there should you be worrying about work. So, give coworkers advance notice, leave a "If you need assistance, contact So-and-So" message in your out-of-office email, and change your voicemail to reflect that you're away.

Real Chick Tip

Don't be afraid to switch careers. Our twenties is a great time to really find out what we love to do—even if that means changing tracks. I used to work in marketing, doing the whole daily grind thing from 9 to 5. But one day, I finally did something I had been wanting to do for awhile: enroll in culinary school. I started taking night classes and loved every second of it. Eventually, I was able to quit my office job to start a new one at an amazing restaurant, as a chef! Although it might seem scary—with a lot of long hours—it's worth it in the end to be able to really do something you enjoy everyday.

−Adrienne, 27, Boston, chef

Ask for progress reports. When your first three months are up, chat with your boss about any issues you might be having with getting adjusted and ask if there's anything you can work on. You're a mature adult and having these conversations are crucial to your success. Do it again after you've been there a year.

Use a study from the European Society of Cardiology as an excuse: working three to four hours of overtime per day is bad for your pretty, little heart. Go home and reboot.

Don't wear miniskirts, too-tight dresses, fishnets, pleather jumpsuits, you get the idea. And avoid cleavage, too. Even if you work in a casual environment, it's important to project yourself as a capable, classy person.

Shake hands. Women are never taught how to give a good handshake. If you're meeting someone new, extend your hand, look him or her in the eye, and shake three times with a firm grip.

Remember your manners. Thank coworkers when they help you with an assignment, bring in a donut for the receptionist when she covered for you when you came in late. Be gracious and appreciative.

Super gross tip ahead: crumbs from snacks that fall into your keyboard can attract vermin at night. Eat away from your computer, and if possible, your desk.

Don't do anything at work that you'd be embarrassed to tell friends or family about.

When it's time to quit, do it as kindly as possibly. You may think you'll never have to work for these people again, but who knows? You could need freelance jobs, or even a full-time one with them again in the future.

Hate public speaking? Take a drop-in acting class.

"LUCK? I DON'T KNOW ANYTHING ABOUT LUCK. I'VE NEVER BANKED ON IT AND I'M AFRAID OF PEOPLE WHO DO. LUCK TO ME IS SOMETHING ELSE: HARD WORK—AND REALIZING WHAT IS OPPORTUNITY AND WHAT ISN'T."
—LUCILLE BALL

ANNND, YOU'RE FIRED.
BUT DON'T WORRY!

Be the bigger person. Regardless of if you've been laid off, axed, or the company has downsized, send your boss a letter thanking them for the experience.

Grab your contacts and run. You can't be escorted out of a building (unless you did something very, very bad and if so, shame on you) so send off a quick email to contacts you were working with, updating them with your new email.

Don't cry. Don't beg. Don't whine and ask "Whyyyy meeee?" because the deed is already done. Keep your cool so they're reminded of how foolish they are for letting you go.

Walk out with your head held high. Stop to hug the people you really enjoyed working with and give them your personal email address so you can stay in touch.

Know your rights. Don't wait to find out if you can continue your health care coverage. Understand what your severance package will be and make sure you use their UPS account to ship your stuff home.

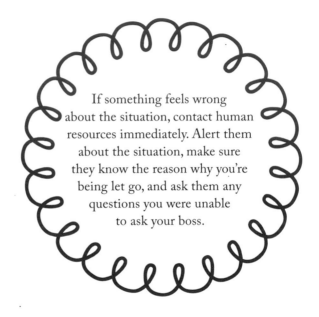

If something feels wrong about the situation, contact human resources immediately. Alert them about the situation, make sure they know the reason why you're being let go, and ask them any questions you were unable to ask your boss.

Don't let it getcha down. Of course it sucks. Of course you feel like a failure. But you're not. Stuff happens. Enjoy a pint of ice cream, cry it out, and wake up the next morning refreshed and ready to start applying for new jobs.

The lack of income and loss of stability is certainly a scary thing. Call your credit card companies, student loans, and any other outstanding bills you have to inform them of the situation and to find out your options until you're on your feet again.

Embrace it sista! Start going to the gym "now that you have time," sign up for a class, read a good book, and apply for jobs you didn't have time to seek out before. Turn your bad situation into a blessing.

Volunteer. If you've wanted a job for a nonprofit but had no experience, now is your chance to break into the field. Offer your services—it's rare for any company to turn down free labor.

HOW TO HANDLE
"FIRED" PROFESSIONALLY

Maria Fuema, Recruiter at Luxe Avenue in NYC, secures talent for mid-management and executive level positions in the luxury and lifestyle sector. Here's her advice on the sticky subject:

1. Don't be hard on yourself, as getting fired can happen to the best of us. Believe in your strengths/skills, in your motivation to advance your career, and in finding the right position for the right reasons.

2. Make sure that it was a legitimate firing and not a wrongful termination. Find out if you are eligible for unemployment benefits before starting your job search.

3. Write a new resumé/cover letter and be sure to emphasize your qualifications—but no need to bring up the circumstances of the firing until you have to, which will probably be at the interview. Therefore, practice and prepare your answers to questions about the firing. Do not lie; most companies check references. Keep it brief and honest, and do not drag your former employer/boss through the mud. Remain diplomatic, respectful, and professional.

4. Even with a clear explanation, you need to be able to convince new employers that you are a "good worker," qualified, motivated, and above all the right fit for the position.

5. Take an objective look and think about what you learned from being fired. Start thinking about what you could have done differently that might have led to another outcome and what you'll do differently in the future/with a prospective employer. Was it a matter of personality clash or your performance? You need to recognize and correct these problems in your next position. Nearly everyone can improve in some area.

ENTERTAINING

"THE ONLY ADVANTAGE OF NOT BEING
TOO GOOD A HOUSEKEEPER IS THAT YOUR
GUESTS ARE SO PLEASED TO FEEL HOW
VERY MUCH BETTER THEY ARE."

—Eleanor Roosevelt

There's only one thing more fun than getting dressed up and going to parties—hosting them. Now we're ignoring the collective moans out there as you imagine how stressful entertaining at home can be. The prep work, the cooking, the guest list, and, worst of all, the clean up. But trust us, becoming a party planning guru is easier than you think. At the very least, we'll teach you how to fake it so every invitee thinks you're a hostess extraordinaire.

THE GUEST LIST

Some people will invite themselves to your party. Often it's best to just let it happen. But if you've got a set of *cajones*, tell them so sorry, but they'll certainly have a spot at your next gathering.

Figure out the purpose of the party. Is it a birthday soirée for yourself? Invite your closest friends to keep it intimate. For more casual gatherings, the invites can be more informal.

When you plan on entertaining, the first order of business is the guest list. Start by looking at your space. Live in a studio apartment? Keep the list from five to ten people. Have a three-bedroom house? Well, we'd cram in everyone we know at that point.

We women tend to focus too much on inclusion and guilt when it comes to parties. But guess what? Not everyone can be invited. Instead, invite the people you want there and if your office buddy finds out and is insulted, let her know you were tight on space and it was anything but personal.

Evites, snail mail, a text . . . Let guests know about the occasion two weeks in advance if it's a theme, one week in advance if it's more formal, and just two days in advance if you're having a casual get-together.

Never invite the following people to a booze fest at your place: your boss, your ex, or your ex's current girlfriend. You might like them now but cocktails can change a person!

PRE-PARTY PLANNING

Once you know who you'd like invited over, the planning can begin. We recommend writing out everything you need to do to prep for guests. Here's a checklist that we always rely on.

THREE DAYS BEFORE

- ❑ Write your grocery list, including food and booze.
- ❑ Confirm who's coming.
- ❑ Plan your outfit (in case there isn't one, in which case, add shopping).

TWO DAYS BEFORE

- ❑ Clean the bathroom. Stock it with extra TP.
- ❑ Take kitchen inventory. Have enough bowls? Platters? Napkins? Glasses? If not, add what you need to pick up to the grocery list.

THE DAY BEFORE

- ❑ Grocery shop.
- ❑ Vacuum, tidy your bedroom, and handle all the cleaning you need to do the night before so the day of the party your home doesn't smell like Mop N' Glo.
- ❑ Make a music playlist. Mix it up with plenty of the top 40, classic tunes, and a few jams from the college years.
- ❑ Make a list of things you forgot to pick up.
- ❑ Get some seltzer and extra paper towels. Someone *will* spill.

THE BIG DAY

- ❏ Do something relaxing, be it a hike, a bike ride, or a face mask.

- ❏ Lay out your outfit. Confirm jewelry, hair and makeup to go along with said outfit.

- ❏ Put out all the booze in one location. Keep a trash bin with a plastic bag next to it to make it easy for guests to recycle (and keep clean up at a minimum).

- ❏ Cook in order of what will take the longest. Putting out chips, cheese, and veggies can be at the last minute.

- ❏ Now pour yourself a cocktail! You're ready to host.

COCKTAILS

Here are four crowd-pleasing drinks that virtually everyone will love. (Be sure to tell guests to BYO if they aren't cocktail fans).

LAURA'S SIGNATURE COCKTAIL: THE SERINO SPRITZER

1 bottle of red wine (merlot or cabernets work well)
1 quart of sparkling lime or lemon water
3–4 cubed peaches
2–3 cubed plums

Fill glasses with fruit and cover with wine, filling glass halfway. Let sit in the fridge for 20 minutes. Top off glasses with sparkling water. You can use any variety of fruit in this concoction. Just add ½ cup of triple sec to make it sangria.

MELISSA'S SIGNATURE COCKTAIL: CANDY GIRL

> Equal parts Malibu Rum and sprite (or 7-Up)
> Sour Skittles or gummy bears (or any other sweet tooth fix you can't live without)

Fill up each glass with the rum and soda. Drop the candy in. A real tough one, eh?

THE BERRY-POLITAN: RECIPE FROM PATRICIA RICHARDS, MASTER MIXOLOGIST AT THE WYNN ENCORE, LAS VEGAS

> 1¾ oz. Ciroc Red Berry Vodka
> ½ oz. Cointreau Liqueur
> ½ oz. freshly squeezed lime juice
> ¾ oz. white cranberry juice
> ¼ oz. simple syrup (1:1 ratio of fine granulated sugar to water, stir to dissolve)
> Garnish: One fresh raspberry, one fresh blueberry, and one slice fresh strawberry, dropped into cocktail.

Method: Combine the above ingredients into a bar mixing glass. Add ice and shake well to chill. Strain into a chilled martini/cocktail glass. Garnish. Serve.

Make sure there are easy snacks out before guests arrive. Go for pretzels, chips, veggies, hummus—anything that can sit out for an hour before friends begin to gather.

THE TWENTYSOMETHING: RECIPE FROM JILLIAN VOSE, DEATH & COMPANY IN NEW YORK CITY

Muddle 6 green grapes in a cocktail shaker and add:

    ½ oz 1:1 simple syrup
    ½ lillet blanc
    ¾ fresh lime juice
    1½ Plymouth gin

Shake with ice and double strain into a cocktail/coupe glass. Garnish with a green grape on a pick.

Not everyone can cook. And that's okay. We're not trying to turn you all into mini Marthas. Start with a menu that you can tackle—especially if you're expecting a larger crowd.

Don't cook something you've never cooked before. This is a disaster waiting to happen. If you always nail baked mac and cheese, serve what you do best. It'll make prepping/cooking/hosting an easier feat.

If you have a small kitchen, stick to apps. If you have an oven that's never been used, stick to apps that don't need to be cooked or thawed.

Once guests have picked away at the starters, wait an hour or so to bring out more food. As drinks are poured, guests will be ready for another round of noshing.

When in doubt, order a few pizzas and cut them up into pieces. Or heat up some frozen plain pizzas and add a different fresh topping to each. Instant crowd pleaser.

Real Chick Tip

Before I had any real experience I agreed to cater a cocktail party for my mother at her Hamptons house—guest list of 150. I decided to make eight types of passed hors d'oeuvres, three kinds of stationary tea sandwiches, a cheese plate, and a passed dessert. I planned ahead as much as I understood to do, but the day before the party, I panicked. What I learned: Limit yourself to two dishes to be served warm (to maximize oven space). Food that can be stored at room temp always should be, and anything that can be put into a compact container until the last minute will help increase fridge space. It's always better to be prepared and lighten your menu so that it's manageable.

–Willy, 25, NYC, caterer

THE MENU

FAST AND DELICIOUS

We've asked chef Candice Kumai, author of *Cook Yourself Sexy* and Iron Chef judge, to share with us two super easy and yummy dishes to serve guests. These will be your future go-tos.

ROASTED FIG + HONEY CHEVRE FLATBREADS

(Excerpt taken from *Cook Yourself Sexy*)

Serves 8, appetizer portions

Ingredients

- 8 fresh figs, tough stem removed and halved
- 1 tablespoon honey
- 2 cups + 1 tablespoon balsamic vinegar
- 1 medium red onion, halved and thinly sliced
- 2 tablespoons extra-virgin olive oil, divided
- 1 store-bought pizza dough
- 4 ounces fresh goat cheese (Chevre)
- 1 cup arugula
- 6 slices prosciutto

Directions

1. Preheat oven to 425°F

2. Toss the figs in a baking dish or sheet tray with 1 tablespoon honey and 1 tablespoon balsamic. Roast for about 15–20 minutes until softened. Cool.

3. Heat the remaining 2 cups balsamic vinegar in a small saucepan over medium-high heat until it comes to gentle boil. Reduce the heat to medium and simmer until the balsamic is reduced to 3/4 cup and has the consistency of maple syrup, about 30 minutes. Cool to room temperature.

4. Heat 2 teaspoons of the olive oil in a large skillet over medium heat. Add the onion and cook, stirring occasionally until the onion is golden, about 10 minutes.

5 Roll out the pizza dough and place on a large sheet tray. Bake at 425°F for about 10–15 minutes until golden brown. Transfer flatbread to a large platter and brush with remaining 1 teaspoon olive oil and a sprinkle of salt. Top with the caramelized onions, figs, goat cheese, arugula, and prosciutto. Drizzle with the balsamic reduction and cut into 16 pieces.

Don't be afraid to ask for some help. If you're serving a big entrée, dole out responsibilities for friends to be in charge of salad and dessert.

SIMPLE SALMON + QUINOA SALAD

(Excerpt taken from www.candicekumai.com)

Ingredients

- 2 cups baby spinach (Easy to purchase in the bag, pre-washed, and adds a vibrant color and major nutrients to any boring ol' salad!)
- 2 cups uncooked quinoa
- 2–5 oz salmon fillet (Frozen fillets are great, convenient and super economical!)
- ¼ cup thinly sliced red onion
- Sea salt to taste
- ¼ cup extra virgin olive oil
- ¼ cup balsamic vinegar
- 1 tablespoon honey

For the easy vinaigrette: Whisk together ¼ cup extra virgin olive oil, ¼ cup balsamic vinegar, and honey

Directions

1. Preheat broiler
2. Bring water to a boil and cook the quinoa, add a bit of salt to taste, strain, and rinse with cold water to stop the cooking process.
3. While quinoa cooks, sprinkle fillet evenly with sea salt. Place fish on a foil-lined broiler pan coated with a drizzle of olive oil. Broil on high for 10 minutes, until fish is opaque and firm to the touch. Gently break the salmon into flaky pieces with a fork and gather in a large mixing bowl.
4. Toss salmon, quinoa, spinach, red onion, and balsamic vinaigrette in a large bowl; toss gently to coat.

AIN'T NO PARTY
LIKE A THEME PARTY

You don't need an occasion to throw a party.
Here are our favorite unique themes to throw, including
what to wear, how to decorate, and what to serve.

PARAZZI PARTY . . .

Have guests either dress as a member of the paparazzi
or as a celebrity that often appears in the tabloids. Set
up a photo booth for staged pictures. Have all guests
sign an autograph book so you remember who came as
what. Serve champagne; celebs only drink the best.

DALLAS PARTY
Channel the '80s smash
with teased hair, shoulder
pads, and cowboy hats.
Charm guests with a
southern accent and hang a
Texas flag.

ABC PARTY . . .

Also known as an "anything but clothes" party. This isn't a show-up-naked party, but an inventive way to have guests craft their own clothing from items like bubble wrap, a cardboard box, or even a shower curtain. Serve very light fare since you don't want any costumes popping off.

MIDDLE AGES PARTY

Encourage guests to dress like their favorite knight, damsel, or court jester. Serve sticks of meat and pour drinks into plastic goblets. Keep the lights dim since there wasn't electricity back in those days.

THE WHITE PARTY

Channel Puff Daddy (also known as P. Diddy, Sean Combs, etc.) and have a summer soirée where guests must wear white. Keep the décor and food all white too: marshmallows, chardonnay, you get the idea.

MOUSTACHE PARTY

Have guests wear their favorite cocktail attire and have felt moustaches for everyone that arrives. Send an invite that reads "I moustache you to join the party." Serve drinks in plastic cups with moustaches drawn on the front.

IMPROMPTU PARTY? NO PROBLEM.

Haley Hogan from Party City lets us know what to keep in stock in case the party ends up at your place.

- A glass container or vase. Use whatever you have on hand to create an instant centerpiece—limes, lemons, or even branches from your yard. A galvanized tub is also great to have on hand if you do lots of outdoor gatherings.

- Cocktail napkins in a fun, seasonal print. Paper towels just don't look as cute when you have guests over.

- Candles. Light them and it instantly creates a warm, cozy environment for visitors.

- Keep a few frozen hors d'oeuvres in the freezer and a tube of cookie mix in the fridge. You'll be able to serve a snack or dessert in an instant.

- A bottle of wine on reserve. If you happen to drink it in desperation one night, replace it!

ENTERTAINING FOR TWO

Studies have shown that men are attracted to comfort flavors and aromas. According to Amy Reiley, author of *Romancing the Stove,* the answer's in peanut butter and fluff. Here's a sure-fire recipe that's both sinful and sweet (and maybe a little sexy, too).

Ingredients

> 1 tablespoon chocolate-flavored peanut butter
> 1½ tablespoon marshmallow fluff*
> 2 slices seeded, whole grain bread
> ½ tablespoon salted butter

Directions

1. Heat a sandwich press. (If you don't have a sandwich press, heat a small frying pan over medium heat.)

2. Butter the outside of both slices of bread. Spread the inside of one slice with the chocolate peanut butter, the other with 1 tablespoon of fluff. Form a sandwich and press until the outside is toasted to golden. If you are using a frying pan, press the sandwich with a large spatula. When one side is golden, flip and repeat. Top the hot sandwich with an additional ½ tablespoon marshmallow fluff. Cut your crispy, toasted sandwich into quarters and serve with extra napkins.

   *My fluff of choice is Ricemallow, a more natural and slightly less sweet mixture, devoid of some of the original's most likely toxic ingredients.

THE CLEAN-UP

Make sure the dishwasher is empty
pre-party. If any bowls of dip or trays
are cleared, rinse and store them in the
dishwasher rather than letting them
pile up in the sink.

Create a "trash triangle" in the party space.
Keep one trash bin by the drinks for empty
bottles and cans, one trash by where the food
is served, and one by the kitchen, which is
the highest traffic area.

If you're using all paper products,
purchase three times the amount of
napkins. Guests tend to grab them
instead of plates and they'll also be handy
if there are crumbs on your dress.

In case of spills, keep bottles of seltzer on display with the other beverages. This way if you aren't around when there's an accident, another guest can spot away a stain.

If you're a total neat freak, roll up the rugs for the night. That way you can just sweep up the mess, rather than worry about stains and vacuuming the next day.

Real Chick Tip

People love mini things. Don't make lasagna, make lasagna cupcakes in muffin tins. Don't serve a seven-layer dip, serve seven-layer dip in shot glasses. Having miniature versions of items makes things easy to eat and they're a lot more fun.

—Sarah E., 28, NYC, food blogger

Your post-party cleaning sesh will be much easier if you casually clean throughout the night. Just don't pull empty plates out of guests' hands . . . that's just rude.

Cleaning wipes. The lazy girls' best friend. We don't encourage using them all the time (not totally eco-friendly) but at the end of the evening, they're great for a wipe on the counters and tables.

Puke happens. Unfortunately, there is always one party guest that might go overboard. If they make it to the bathroom, bravo. If they don't, blot with white vinegar and cut them off.

Forgot to put away a bottle of bubbly? Plop a raisin or dried cranberry into the bottle to reactivate the fizz and make a morning after mimosa.

As desperate as you'll be to just hit your bed at the end of the night, at the very least make sure food goes back in the fridge. Otherwise you'll be waking up to a stinky situation.

ETIQUETTE

"MANNERS ARE A SENSITIVE AWARENESS
OF THE FEELINGS OF OTHERS. IF YOU HAVE
THAT AWARENESS, YOU HAVE GOOD MANNERS,
NO MATTER WHAT FORK YOU USE."

—*Emily Post*

Gossip Girls (R.I.P.), Pretty Little Liars . . . any of *The Real House-wives* franchises. Fictional or non, we're flooded with displays of manners gone bad on a daily basis. And that's not just on TV. Think of all those times during the workweek when the rumor mill reaches your desk, or you hear about arguments and embarrassing scandals in the news. Poor politesse is everywhere!

But you mind your Ps and Qs, right? Truth is, any successful role model will tell you that proper etiquette is vital for a fruitful future. So before you lose your cool in uber uncomfortable situations, take a breath and remind yourself you're a lady. The basics aside (we're assuming you know to say 'thanks'), here's the 4-1-1 on issues we hear about the most in this age range.

WHAT TO DO OR NOT DO, A CRASH COURSE

Regarding funeral wear, think subdued colors and dress up. A plain black, navy blue, or brown shift dress and solid toned cardigan is a safe bet, or a dark blouse and skirt sans patterns. Avoid high heels or shoes that will make noise. And denim (we don't care if it's dark) is never okay.

Silverware is arranged by the order of its use. Start at the far left and work your way in.

Keep the captive audience in your elevator ride happy: no phone calls 'til you're off.

Don't wear white to a wedding. Unless you're the bride. Or unless you're Pippa Middleton.

For god's sakes, cover your mouth when you yawn. There's no need to share your morning breath. Gross.

Ever forget if your bread dish and drink is to the left or right of you? Use a little sign language, making a lowercase 'b' with your left hand and a lowercase 'd' with your right. (b for bread, left; d for drink, right)

If you're sitting down when a pal introduces you to a person who is standing, stand up.

Respond to an invitation as soon as humanly possible. If you get one in the mail, leave it in plain sight until you know whether or not you can attend, then answer it stat.

Here's the rule on hostess gifts: If you think she's spending money on you, do the same. For example, a casual movie night doesn't require a gift, but be sure to bring a dessert or wine when invited to a dinner party.

When you're emailing someone you don't know personally, always use Mr. or Ms. and the last name. In follow up emails, address them the same way they signed their name in their email back to you.

It's fine to head back to your desk while your lunch is nuking in the office microwave, but don't forget and return five minutes past the buzz. That's a fast track to having someone be annoyed with you. The same etiquette applies to the laundromat.

When it comes to wedding gifts you don't have a year to send a gift to the happy couple. Bring it to the wedding or ship it to the couple's home beforehand.

Sneeze and cough into the crook of your arm, *not* your hands. And turn away when you do.

If you're at a fundraiser or charity event and happen to win the 50/50 raffle, it's customary to donate your winnings on the spot to the cause at hand.

Don't talk on the phone in restaurants, theatres, trains, buses, libraries, spas, and anywhere with a "No Cell Phone" sign. You don't want to hear about someone else's failed relationship on a two-hour Amtrak ride, and no wants to hear about yours.

Mid-mani/pedi, you're typically asked to pay. You should also tip during this time, too, so your manicurist isn't left to wonder the rest of time if and how much you're tipping.

When it comes to receiving gifts—housewarming, engagement, shower, what have you—tradition holds true, even in modern times: Write out a sincere thank you note and mail it. Don't listen to anyone who says you have a year. Three months is acceptable, but ASAP is better.

LET'S TALK ABOUT TIPPING

Being strapped for cash isn't a reason to ditch tipping, but you also don't have to 1) tip like Oprah, or 2) tip for every service. So what do you do when you're unsure how much to leave, if anything? No better person to ask than Lizzie Post, great-great-granddaughter of the one and only Emily Post, and co-author of *Emily Post's Etiquette 18th Edition* as well as *How Do You Work This Life Thing?* When in doubt, ask someone ahead of time at the establishment (like a receptionist). It's as simple as: "I'm sorry, I'm new to this situation. Is it customary to tip for . . . ?" Or, reference Post's tip sheet below, which can be found in full at EmilyPost.com.

Bartender: $1 to $2 per drink or 15% to 20% of the tab.

Bellhop: $2 for the first bag, $1 for each one after that.

Cable people: No need to tip them or repairmen, that's their job.

Food delivery: 10% to 15% of the bill.

Gas station attendant: No need if they just fill the tank. If they wash the windows, too, give around a dollar.

Hair stylists: 15% to 20%; ask it to be split if you had more than one person help you.

Hotel housekeeper: $2 to $5 daily in an envelope marked "housekeeping."

Manicurist, masseuse, facial or waxing specialist: 15% to 20%.

Movers: Tip when the job is complete. Head mover: between $25 and $50; crew members between $15 and $30 each, dependent on how much they moved, care they've taken, and difficulty. If they've packed your belongings, too, increase the amount.

Take out: This one is up to you. No need, unless it's a really complicated order or you did curbside service.

Taxi driver: 15% to 20% of the fare.

Wait service: 15% to 20%, before tax (even if you have a coupon).

Real Chick Tip

"Dressing in skimpy clothes may not be a big deal back home, but in other countries, it sends out a different message and casts attention on you. While traveling abroad, carry a light scarf or shawl in your bag. When I visited a basilica in Florence, women were not permitted to enter if their shoulders weren't covered. Women also don't wear short shorts in most other countries."

–Emily, 27, TX,
blogger at maiden-voyage-travel.com

WHO ORDERED THE
SIX SHOTS OF SAKE?

The scene. Picture this: You agree to dinner with friends (let's say sushi), intending only to spend a little bit on your meal. Before long, others have ordered sake shots, bottles of wine, a gazillion special rolls topped with caviar . . . and then the bill comes. And someone decrees, "Let's just split it." Sound familiar? We posed this common conundrum to Jacqueline Whitmore, international etiquette expert and author of *Poised for Success*, and here's what she said.

The solution. "If you feel that your portion of the bill is substantially lower and/or you'd rather not split the check, speak up. The time to do this is before the server takes your order ('Do you mind if we get separate checks?'). However, if you missed the opportunity, say something when the check arrives. 'John, I'd love to split the bill, but I brought just enough cash to pay for my own meal. Why don't we split it the next time?' Or if you plan to pay with a credit card you can say, 'John, since I didn't eat much, I prefer to pay for my own meal. Why don't we split the check the next time around?' Next time, you may even want to discreetly ask the server for a separate check.

One of Bridezilla's six matching minions? Here's the dealio: It's her day. Try to do what she says. And wear whatever she selects—no questions asked. However, if you can't afford to attend an event or be a bridesmaid, be honest and say so.

DEALING WITH PEOPLE . . . ANNOYING OR OTHERWISE

EXCUSE ME, BUT I BELIEVE THAT WAS MY IDEA!

When the office diva blatantly pitches your genius idea as her own, first reaction is to talk smack with your cube crew—but hold that thought. Founder of TheGraciousGirl.net and a well-mannered alumna of the Protocol School of Washington, Mindy Lockard, has a better plan:

1. Resolve to be graciously upfront with her. Spreading gossip creates more office drama and doesn't reflect well on yourself.

2. Map it out on paper. What do you think happened, what will you say, and what are you hoping to get out of being honest with her? Keep in mind that if you're looking for an apology and you don't get one, you might get even angrier.

3. Confront her with humility, without seeming defensive. A few talking points:

   a. I noticed you pitched an idea . . .

   b. This is what I felt . . .

   c. It's bothering me a little bit that . . .

   d. Maybe I'm not understanding it right . . .

   e. Could you explain to me what happened . . .

4. Then stop, and let her fill the silence.

5. Moving forward, share your great ideas with the right people, and maybe vow that that's the last time you share it over lunch or a cocktail—without others around to prove it was yours.

So your boyfriend's mother is the queen of backhanded compliments? The next time she tosses one your way, tell her a story about something nice her son did for you and that she did a wonderful job raising a good man. She should get the hint.

Your friends got engaged, woohoo! If you'd like, send them a congratulatory card in the mail. If they invite you to an engagement party, that's when you can give a gift—even if they say not to bring any.

Gotta love dear old Grandma Maude—except when she asks you, for the gazillionth time, when you're getting married (or having a baby, and so on). Answer: "I'm so enjoying my career right now, but I'm excited for that chapter of my life, too, whenever it begins!"

When that ripped lady in the sports bra surpasses your gym's time limit and shows no sign of ditching her treadmill, you have a choice: confront her, or tell an employee. We asked a few gym staffers and survey says: Go the employee route, so it's a matter of gym policy, not confrontation.

Ah, the one night stand. If you get up first and want to peace out, leave a note saying "It was nice to meet you." Interested in a second round? Then leave your number, too.

So your coworker, aunt, friend's mom, or hair stylist wants to set you up? And you're not feeling it? Tell them to hold that thought for another time; that you've got a lot of other things to focus on for now but may tap their resources in the future. It's better to keep all doors open rather than closed.

In the workplace, it's crucial to stay calm. If you find yourself desperately trying to bite your tongue, take a five-minute fresh air break and return with a cool head.

Sometimes, running into your ex is simply unavoidable—like at a mutual friend's wedding or party. Regardless of how horrific the breakup was, act like the cool cat he first fell for so he'll leave with only fond memories of you. If you feel the urge to cry, pick a fight, or stare, then leave the room.

Same goes for meeting your current man's ex-girl. Remember, he's yours now. Be nice, but no need to act fake and try to be her best friend.

It's been fifteen minutes and your server still hasn't brought the honey mustard you requested, which you need in order to enjoy your sandwich. Next time she flies by, catch her eye and say, "Busy night, huh? Sorry to add on to it, but think you could bring that honey mustard next time you pass by?" Kill 'em with kindness; always works.

If someone asks to try your drink and you're a huge germophobe, say you don't mean to be a pain but the last time you shared you caught a bug—so your new policy is to decline.

THE LIFE AND TIMES OF LIVING WITH A ROOMMATE.

She uses your stuff. She rarely cleans up her own messes. She has her boyfriend over so often, he may as well pay a third of the rent. What to do? We picked Lizzie Post's brain on this one, too, and she told us about the three C's . . .

COMMUNICATION. Ideally, the following convo is best had when you first move in, but it's never too late to have it. Sit down with her to chat about the fact that during your cohabitation, there's potential for problems to crop up. Ask what the best way to approach her is when this happens, and in return, tell her you want to know immediately and directly if something is bothering her; harboring grudges causes friendships to dissolve fast. Maybe agree to say something like, "We need to have a roommate talk," when these times pop up, acknowledging that isn't meant to offend the other person.

COMPROMISE. Find middle ground while being as polite as possible. Post demonstrated with this sample convo: "Hey, Jenny. This isn't easy to bring up, but I'm starting to feel like Frank is spending a lot of time here. I really like him and I'm so excited for your relationship, but I do need a little space sometimes. Is there another place you guys could hang out, or maybe we could pick a few nights a week when it will just be us two?"

COMMITMENT. During your initial talk about how you'll address difficult situations, also agree that it should be protocol to check in on each problem say, a month after the compromise chat. Example: "I definitely know I need to clean my kitchen messes better, and you'll work on the living room. Let's chat about it again in a month and see how we're doing!" See? Easy, peasy, and no one loses any teeth in the process.

INTERNET OVERLOAD

If you search "what's the proper etiquette for," over 14,900,000 results pop up. This guide is a little easier to navigate.

THE PROPER ETIQUETTE FOR ...

Not attending a wedding ...
Send a gift anyway, if you were invited.

Buying a wedding gift ...
Either stay on the registry or give money. The amount should reflect how much you think your meal is costing the couple.

Attending a potluck ...
Make enough for at least two thirds of the guest list. Be mindful of potential food allergies out there by jotting down the ingredients on an index card.

Free makeovers in the cosmetic department . . .
If you know flat out you're not buying anything,
don't waste her time and take her away from actual
buying customers. But if you're open to the idea, go
ahead and ask for an application. If in the end you
decide not to buy, at least ask her to write down your
favorite product that she used, suggesting you'll be
back for it another time.

Meeting your friends' newborn baby...
Rather than ask to hold their baby, wait for them
to ask if you want to. If you'd like to bring a gift,
ask them if there's anything they still need.
(When in doubt, buy a book). And if the little
rugrat is sleeping, let him or her be—for the
parents' sake.

When the server pours you the first glass of wine . . .
Note the label on the bottle to be sure it's what you
ordered. Swirl, smell, taste, and nod in approval.
If he places the cork next to you, it's so that
you can notice its condition. If there's mold
or it's too dry, let him know.

LESSONS FROM A CUSTOMER SERVICE GURU

In the trenches of one of today's hottest e-tailers lies a customer service specialist who fields questions by the minute, tweets with clientele (@RueLaLa_help), and puts out fires left and right—all while keeping chic and composed. Amy Bootier, Rue La La Concierge, applies what she's learned in her rollercoaster line of biz to everyday life and shares those tips here:

1. Be nice to everyone You just never know. The person at the other end of the phone, or the owner of that Twitter handle, or at that party, is a potential employer, a networking opportunity, or eventually a best friend. Save yourself the foot-in-digital-mouth moments.

2. Keep an eye on the Big Picture This will help in situations that could get blown out of proportion to stay cool and in perspective, but give bigger things their due process.

3. Know when to pull the plug We've all had that black-hole friendship, major, or job: you sink time, energy, and resources into it, to get nothing in return. Sometimes you just need to figure out if the juice is worth the squeeze, and start issuing DNRs.

4. Being right and doing the right thing aren't always the same Sure, you could spend your days pointing out fine print and semantics and building a case for your rightness, but eventually no one will want to be around you. Learn when to take the hit, suck it up, and apologize.

5. Listen to what's being said, not what you want to hear If people realize they're not being heard, they'll move on to someone who will genuinely listen.

Real Chick Tip

When in public, be considerate of the people around you. Lower your voice, put your phone on vibrate, and avoid pounding on your laptop keyboard. I once held a job that required me to commute for two hours on Amtrak—there and back, daily—and quickly learned how many people don't do this. Not only did they form eternal enemies up and down the aisle, they were inevitably booted from the early morning quiet car. Imagine how embarrassing? Now whenever I ride the train, I stay as quiet as humanly possible. And yell at those who aren't.

–AnneMarie, 29, NY, buyer

FASHION

"I DON'T KNOW WHO INVENTED HIGH HEELS,
BUT ALL WOMEN OWE HIM A LOT."

—*Marilyn Monroe*

When it comes to fashion in your twenties, there really are no rules. It's a great decade to be able to get away with even the quickest fads (i.e. harem pants) and discover your personal style. Even if you don't consider yourself a fashionista, being mindful of dressing correctly is something every gal should learn. Gone are the college days of wearing sweatpants in daylight. Your twenties are the perfect time to break bad habits and embrace new ones. It's also a great time to build a well-curated wardrobe, hopefully on a budget, with a focus on classics you'll love for a long time.

THE BASICS—WHAT YOU NEED IN YOUR CLOSET

A white oxford shirt is versatile enough to wear to work or dress down with jeans. Invest in a crisp cotton poplin that will last.

Black three-inch pumps with a round toe will make your legs look a mile long, guaranteed. Get a pair you can walk in comfortably. These go with everything from jeans to a pencil skirt to a sequin cocktail dress.

Get yourself a pair of slim leg jeans. Sure, there are skinnies, flares, boot cut—but a straight leg is always in style. A darker wash is more multipurpose and can easily be dressed up.

V-neck tee's are the most handy things you'll own. Keep three in your rotation: gray, white, and black. You will wear them more than you can ever know.

A pair of animal print flats may not sound like a staple, but on days where your wardrobe is a bit bland, it's an effortless way to give it a little *rawr*.

Something with sequins— whether it's a pair of flats, a mini skirt, or a tank— there is always a time and place for extra glitz. New Years Eve, bachelorette party, club opening, or hey, a fancy night at home.

The any-weather trench is an instant way to look chic—even if you're rocking a sweatshirt underneath. Hell, it even looks good with nothing underneath.

The little black dress. It doesn't matter what the silhouette, shape, or brand is—just make sure it fits you like a glove. Invest in one that will forever remain in your rotation.

Fit is everything. Wearing clothes that flatter your figure and make you feel comfortable is half the battle in your quest for fashion fierceness.

FINDING YOUR PERSONAL STYLE

Use sites like pinterest.com or polyvore.com to document styles you love, and keep a binder of magazine clippings that intrigue you. Instant inspiration when you can't figure out what to wear.

"STYLE IS A WAY TO SAY WHO YOU ARE WITHOUT HAVING TO SPEAK." —RACHEL ZOE

Don't let your lifestyle dictate how you dress. If you work in a hospital and are used to sporting scrubs, that doesn't mean you can't invest in a pair of red high heels that will make you feel sexy on the weekend.

Love something but insist it's "not you"? That's poppycock. If you're afraid to dress like the woman you want to be, you're holding yourself back from becoming the woman you want to be. Be bold.

Break out of your comfort zone. If you reach for the same black tops for a night on the town, force yourself into something different. Sometimes taking a leap can change your mind about what you think you can wear.

A colorful pencil skirt. We've all heard that we need one of these—and it turns out we do. But forget the basic black and gray and go with a bold purple or bright teal. Just keep the shoes and shirt toned down.

That said, know your body. If you wear a size DD bra and skinny suspenders are back in, you might want to avoid that trend altogether. We don't care how much you love it.

Be mindful of feeling comfortable. Your style gut will tell you when something isn't right. If you're uncomfortable in an outfit in front of your bedroom mirror, you'll sure as hell be uncomfortable in it when you leave the house.

DEALING WITH TRENDS

When it comes to trends, be realistic. If it's a fad you love but just know won't last, invest in just one piece and try to get it for a bargain. Affordable stores like Forever 21 are a good starting place.

Keep the balance. If you're constantly chasing the trends, you'll have no time to develop your own personal style.

Don't become a maniac over the mania. If you're okay with waiting five hours in line for Target's newest designer collaboration, that's on you. But those are five hours you'll never get back.

If you're wondering if you're too old for it, you probably are.

Fashtastrophe: *noun. A fashion term coined by Toni Ferrara that means "a fashion catastophe"*

DENIM HEAVEN

Toni Ferrara, celebrity stylist, offers her expert insight on fashion's greatest triumph: jeans.

- **Go dark.** Regardless of your shape or size, there's a brand of dark skinny jeans that are right for you. They're versatile to dress up or down and they create a slim silhouette on anyone.

- **Make it personal.** Don't pay attention to trends, but on the styles you feel best in. Keep the classics on hand in a dark wash straight leg and a lighter color for spring and summer.

- **Find the perfect fit.** Pay attention to how jeans fit in the hips and bottom first. If it's loose in the waist, it can be tailored.

- **Size ain't nuthin' but a number.** After all, only you'll know the size. Don't try to squeeze into a smaller size. The only place a muffin top is welcomed is at breakfast.

- **Avoid the extremes.** Super low cuts the torso at an unappealing place and a super high waist will make you appear thicker. Let's leave those two jean fashtastophes in the past.

CLOSET UPKEEP

Keep a constant inventory of your closet. If you see a pair of jeans you "can't live without" but you already own fifteen pairs, purge before your splurge.

Don't organize by color. It never works. Plus, who wants to see how much black they really own? Embarrassing . . .

Save room by folding jeans, sweaters, and tees rather than storing them on hangers.

Real Chick Tip

My biggest fashion faux pas had to be low-rise jeans. Even my dad called me a plumber. I also had a belt obsession but having a large chest and short waist just made me look like I had a thorax. Now I know better and aim for skinny belts and flowy shirts so I create a waist and don't look like an ant. It's all about figuring out what looks right on your body.

–Eileen, 28, Chicago, entrepreneur

Snow outside doesn't mean you need to box up your summer dresses. Wear lined tights and layer sweaters or button-downs over warm weather frocks to instantly update them for winter.

Rotate your closet by season. In the winter, pull your sweaters and wool skirts to the front. Move them to the back as the weather heats up.

Treat accessories as you do your clothes. Hang clutches, belts, and favorite necklaces from hangers so they're all at eye level and not in a pile on the floor.

Bins. We kinda hate them. Why? Things are stored but they're harder to see. Instead, use hanging shelves so you can easily view your collection.

Garment racks are a girl's best friend. If your modest apartment has a pint-size closet, a rolling rack is a great way to corral favorites in the open. Just make sure they're neatly arranged. Find them at your local Target or Wal-mart.

If you don't even have the space to add a garment rack, then your goal should be to have a carefully cultivated closet of items you really love. That should be every gal's goal in the end.

BE A SMART SHOPPER

Set a budget. Whether it's a weekly, monthly, or yearly allowance, pay attention to how much you spend on clothes. The more aware you are, the smarter you'll shop.

Check out your favorite websites the week before a national holiday (Memorial Day, Martin Luther King Jr., etc.). Sites are always looking to promote a sale around that time.

For the stuff you wear on a daily basis, go for quality. It's better to drop $150 on a pair of jeans that will last instead of spending $50 a month on pieces on sale.

Get on the email list of your favorite brands. You'll be the first to know about sales, new arrivals, and markdowns.

Check out those racks! The clearance ones. They should always be the first place you look when you're in a store.

Use shopping tools like beso.com and shopstyle.com to refine shopping results by price, size, and color to find exactly what you want for the right price. These sites will sort hundreds of ecommerce shops for you.

Speaking of sample sales—they're rarely a good idea. Unless it's for a designer you're familiar with, don't get caught up in the chaos surrounding them. You'll end up spending money on something that you don't really love.

Pay attention to customer reviews. Insight from girls that have already purchased an item can tell you a lot about size, color, and overall quality.

Real Chick Tip

Don't sacrifice your comfort for fashion. You can be stylish and comfortably dressed at the same time! When you don't have to fuss over what you wear you just carry yourself differently, with more confidence. Confidence is probably the best fashion accessory that money can't buy. It's the key ingredient for being able to pull off any look.

−Ashley, 23, fashion blogger,
Milkteeths.blogspot.com

VYING FOR VINTAGE

What better way to add a little pizzazz to your wardrobe than with vintage clothes? Carrie Peterson, founder of Beacon's Closet in New York City, shows us how to get started.

- Start at a local thrift store or Goodwill. Look for something that fits your aesthetic since you don't want to look costumey.

- Pay attention to sizing. A vintage size 12 for example is comparable to a modern size 6.

- Try to limit yourself to only wearing 3 pieces of vintage at a time, max. A vintage dress is great, but pair it with a modern shoe.

- Pay attention to care labels if they're still intact. If you're unsure of the fabric or how to wash a piece, visit your local dry cleaners and ask.

- No vintage shops in your town? Start with eBay and beaconscloset.com, of course.

- If you have the budget for just one vintage piece, choose a jacket or purse. They're easy to throw on and add instant style to any outfit.

Buy what fits. Desperate to squeeze into that skirt you found at a sample sale because it's only $40? Take that $40 and find one that fits.

Think about how you get dressed in the morning and organize accordingly. Do you start with a top and work around that? Make sure they're front and center. Do you start with shoes? Then store those stilettos center stage.

Love designer but live like a pauper? Sign up for free accounts at ruelala.com, ideeli.com, gilt.com, and beyondtherack.com. These online boutiques peddle haute couture at seriously discounted prices, and when you refer a click-happy friend who makes a purchase, you'll score up to $25 of free credit.

WHAT TO WEAR

Having a morning meltdown before a big day? Here are surefire outfits you'll want in your arsenal.

ON AN INTERVIEW . . .

A white button-down, colored pencil skirt, and black pumps. Keep the accessories minimal: a great pair of studs or a pretty silk scarf.

A FIRST DATE—AND YOU DON'T KNOW WHAT'S PLANNED . . .

Dark jeans, a dressy tee or tank (silk or jersey), cardigan, and flats. Keep the top looser in case a spaghetti dinner is in order and always, always avoid heels. You don't want to complain about your achy feet on the first encounter.

A COCKTAIL PARTY FOR WORK . . .

The little black dress. But not too little. You'll look reserved and professional, and if you spill red wine, you're covered.

A COCKTAIL PARTY FOR FRIENDS . . .

Jeans and a sequin top. There isn't always a great reason to wear sequins, but this is one of them. Carry a large enough purse in case you want to sneak in a flask.

GIRL'S NIGHT . . .

Staying in? Your favorite college tee and jeans. Headed out? Your favorite college jeans and anything but a tee.

AN IMPROMPTU DINNER WITH FRIENDS . . .

A striped tee and floral or brightly colored pants. You'll be an instant conversation starter and surprise!—that combo actually works.

MEETING THE PARENTS...

Your favorite outfit—whatever it is, within reason. The more comfortable you feel, the more at ease you'll be. If it includes a leopard print halter however, you may want to rethink this advice.

WHAT NOT TO WEAR . . . EVER

Leggings as pants with a short top. We don't care how perky your bum is, if you're wearing leggings, make sure your top is falling at the knee or below.

Tattered sweatpants outside of the home. Let's keep some dignity intact.

A thong on display. There's nothing wrong with wearing thongs. In fact, we encourage that. But if it's peeking out of your pants, don't leave the house.

Pajama pants during the day. Unless you're still in college. That's acceptable.

Fur on anything other than outerwear. Boots and bags that look like they came off the abominable snowman are a no go.

Socks with sandals. Any time this trend returns, it's very fleeting. Best to avoid it altogether.

Shorts that reveal any part of your butt cheeks. Again, we don't care how perky it is, put it away.

Real Chick Tip

Denim is the most important piece in my closet. In college, it was worn almost everyday, in the form of jeans, shorts, or skirts (some shorter than I may want to remember) and after college it was what I had to wear every single day for my first "real" job. I then learned to get creative with it. Dark jeans can dress up a basic t-shirt, a chambray shirt can dress down the fanciest item of clothing. It has always been a go-to for comfort on the weekends and we all have a pair that just make us feel good on a bad day. Now I wear denim in more ways than ever (vest, jacket, chambrays, jeans, shorts), but I know better than to wear them too tight or too short cause that sure is not sexy.

−Ashley, 27, ME, stylist and blogger of ohsweetwilliam.com

Platform sneakers or sandals. Unless you're the next Spice Girl, in which case, congrats!

 Chokers. They cover the sexiest part of a woman. Stick to necklaces that elongate the neck or skim the collarbone.

A men's button down as a dress. There are very few women that can pull this off. And by very few, we mean four—and they're all Victoria's Secret models.

Running shoes when you're not running. We don't care how comfortable these are and if you're "just wearing them on your walk to work." Flats exist for a reason, ladies.

WHAT TO WEAR . . . UNDER THERE

La Perla's Director of Retail Jenny Holmes weighs in on what we should be wearing underneath it all—plus, how to shop and care for it, too.

1. Start fresh. Before you go for a fitting, toss out every bra that's beat up and worn.

2. Don't assume you know your size. The worst mistake is to assume you're a 34B and ask for that size. Head to your nearest lingerie store and get measured by a professional. The results will surprise you.

3. Every bra fits differently so make sure you try on different sizes depending on if it's a sheer style or a push-up.

4. Every lady should own three everyday bras and three that are more fun and sexy. The style will depend on what fits you best.

5. Never wear the same bra two days in a row. They need rest to maintain their shape.

6. Wash bras every two weeks by hand so they last longer.

7. Every girl needs thongs to wear for the everyday and comfortable boy shorts to sleep in. Try high-waisted, seamless briefs to wear under a skirt.

8. There is no such thing as a lingerie faux pas. As long as you're comfortable in what you're wearing, you're ready for bed.

FOOD & DRINK

"I COME FROM A FAMILY WHERE GRAVY IS
CONSIDERED A BEVERAGE."

—*Erma Bombeck*

Mangia! Venez manger! Comer! Eat more! Regardless of how your grandmother said it to you growing up, food and drink is an integral part of any healthy (and happy) twentysomething's life. We're less focused on the latest fad diet or how to cook like Julia Child. Instead, we want to know how we can snack healthier, when we should clean out our fridge, and how the heck to know if we should be a vegetarian or not. When it comes to eating and drinking, we have quite the appetite. After all, the way to a woman's heart is through her stomach.

BREAKFAST MADE EASY

It's the most important meal of the day, so don't skip out on it (doing so actually puts you at greater risk of gaining weight). Even if it means a banana or cereal bar on the run, make sure you fuel up before your day begins.

Smoothies are awesome, but they can take time and make a mess in the morning. Instead, make them the night before.

Take a few minutes to chop up a bunch
of veggies—red pepper, green pepper,
onion, mushrooms—and toss them all
into a plastic container in the fridge.
Make an omelet in minutes by sprinkling
the mixture onto eggs in the morning.

Frozen waffles are the bomb.
Just make sure you pick a
whole-grain brand, not a
fatty Eggo.

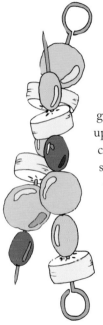

Fruit kabobs! Slide some
grapes, banana, and chopped
up melon onto a skewer. You
can drive, walk, or take the
subway and eat at the same
time. Just be careful not to
poke someone.

Switch to skim. If you can't part with
your morning macchiato, you can cut
almost seventy calories if you swap your
whole milk for non-fat.

Whole wheat wrap, plus one
egg, and black beans—delish.

Whole wheat cereal or oatmeal in packets takes just a minute in the microwave. Plus they're filling and packed with vitamins and iron.

Bagels and muffins are not all bad—if you eat them in moderation. Keep them low-fat and avoid any sugary additions, like chocolate chips.

Try a banana breakfast sandwich. Slice it in half and smear on peanut butter topped with raisins. Put it back together so you can eat it on the go.

Make a tub of Greek yogurt your new best friend. One scoop of that topped off with any fruit of your choice. Totally filling and delicious.

You can still eat cereal even if you're an adult. Choose a brand that has lots of fiber (it's good for you) and isn't sugar-centric (no Frosted Flakes).

LUNCH MADE SIMPLE

Some dieticians say five small deals a day—others suggest there's nothing wrong with a big lunch and no snacks. Pick something that suits your workday and whatever best fits your schedule.

Have a TCT: Turkey, cheese, and tomato. It's protein, veggies, and dairy in one.

Embrace leftovers. If you're making a meal for dinner, try to portion enough so it can double as lunch the next day.

Remember Lunchables as a kid? Well, they're actually not so tasty as an adult (we sampled some), but the idea is great: fill up a Tupperware with sliced meats, cheese, apple slices, and crackers.

Stockpile salads. Sure the salad bar has all the toppings you could ever want, but it can cost a pretty penny. Instead buy all your ingredients—chickpeas, alfalfa spouts, beets, the works—and portion out salads on a Sunday night to have for the week.

Behold the power of a whole-wheat pita. Fill it with virtually anything from hummus and cucumbers to peanut butter and bananas.

Check out the cartons of soup in your organic food aisle. They're cheap (under $5) and you can pour portions into a container for lunch and put it back in the fridge to use again.

Strawberry and cream cheese sandwich. Sounds weird, we know, but try it. It's less than 130 calories and is totally yum.

Grill some chicken breasts ahead of time and slice into strips—or look for pre-cooked chicken in the market if you're always short on time. The protein is important for midday and you can use it on a sandwich, in a salad, or eaten alone with a balsamic drizzle.

Use mesclun greens or spinach as your base and make a "garbage" salad. Use any leftovers you have in your fridge: from taco toppings to leftover penne.

Couscous and quinoa are great bases. Cook it the night before with your favorite add-ins and eat it cold the next day.

When in doubt, a PB&J is a girl's best friend. But consider trying Better'n Peanut Butter (look in the all-natural aisle) and jams with reduced sugar.

BYOL as much as possible so you can control your portions and calories. And if you're eating out, don't be afraid to ask for a healthy suggestion from your waiter. (And if you're going the fast food route, see our healthy picks below.)

FAST FOOD DONE RIGHT

Need something sweet? Most fast food chains have soft serve. Choose their low-fat option but hey, if you're doing well with the salads, you might as well splurge on dessert.

Craving McDonalds? Opt for their grilled chicken classic—no fries, skip the soda. Instead try their Iced Tea.

Desperate for a burger? Go for the Jr. at Wendy's and resist the sides.

If you're getting your Jared on at a Subway, choose the Deli Style Turkey Breast sandwich or a salad. Just nix the packaged dressing (it's loaded with calories).

Go "fresco style" at Taco Bell so you'll get fresh salsa instead of the cheese and sauce combo.

Even though it's sacrilege, opt for grilled (not fried) chicken on a jaunt to KFC. Choose a side of veggie over mashed potatoes and gravy.

ON-THE-GO SNACKING

We know you're always on the move. But rather than duck into a fast-food restaurant when you're jonesing for something to nosh on, Isabel De Los Rios, nutritionist and cofounder of *Beyond Diet*, gives us the best snacks that are easy to pack with you and won't pack on the pounds.

- Make your own trail mix using raw almonds, pumpkin seeds, and dried berries.

- Keep it simple by tossing an orange, apple, or banana in your bag. They don't need refrigeration so they're easy to throw in your purse.

- An almond butter sandwich on sprouted grain bread gives you a great dose of fiber and protein and will fill you up. Or spread some on crackers and toss them in a to-go baggie.

- Take canned fish and crackers with you. It's a great snack or lunch option in a pinch. Opt for rice or spelt crackers.

- Greek yogurt (choose one with no added sugar) topped with raw walnuts and a drizzle of honey.

- Dried apple rings, dried pears, papaya, and mango are incredibly delicious and will curb your afternoon cravings for sweets.

DINNER IN A FLASH

Write out a list of dinner ideas for the week and try your best to stick to it.

Check out supercook.com where you can plug in what you have in your fridge; they'll suggest recipes with the ingredients you've got.

Set aside a little grocery cash each week for something new and different. Add to your already existing array of the basics and it might inspire a creative pursuit in the kitchen. (Hint: lasagna noodles, polenta, bok choy—something you wouldn't normally pick up).

Keep a recipe binder by the fridge and organize by ingredient. For example, chicken, beef, pasta. You can cook based on what you have on hand, rather than flipping through recipes to try and figure out what you can whip up.

If you're in a dinner rut (you cook the same five things over and over again) hop on to a few food blogs for inspiration. We love smittenkitchen. com and 101cookbooks.com.

Pick a tried-and-true veggie and think of a new way to cook it. (Broil brussell sprouts or grill zucchinis.)

Invest in a slow cooker. Once you set it and forget it once, you'll never look back.

Real Chick Tip

I hate going to a restaurant and seeing my favorite bottle of wine listed for four times the price I pay at the store. Call ahead to see if the restaurant has a corkage fee. These usually range from $5–$20, but it's usually a better deal than buying a bottle once you're there, especially if your dining with a large party and you know you will be having several.

–Meagan S., 29, NY, copywriter

20 MEALS FOR UNDER $20

MEXICAN WRAPS
One box of rice + one can of
beans + one tortilla

BREAKFAST FOR DINNER
Two eggs + sweet potatoes +
onion + sausage links

CHICKEN AND BROCCOLI
Chicken breasts seasoned in the
oven + broccoli steamed + box
of rice pilaf

TLT
Sliced tempeh + lettuce +
tomato + whole wheat bread

HEALTHY SALAD
One bag of salad + avocado +
tomato + onion + can of beets

PIZZA
Pizza dough + jar of sauce +
pepperoni stick + green pepper
+ onion

QUICHE
Milk + eggs + butter +
grated cheese + a frozen
veg + pie crust

VEGGIE PASTA
Penne + yellow pepper + red pepper + red onion + lemon and olive oil.

STUFFED SQUASH
One acorn squash stuffed with + couscous + cranberries + chopped almonds

EASY QUINOA
Two cups of quinoa + grilled zucchini + crumbled goat cheese + pine nuts

PASTA VERDE
Gemelli pasta + zucchini + snap peas + baby spinach

CAPRESE SANDWICH
Mozzarella + tomato + basil + baguette

MEDITERRANEAN MEDLEY
Pita chips + hummus + sliced up veggies

SHRIMP SCAMPI PASTA
Linguine + Shrimp + dash of Rosemary

CHICKEN STIR-FRY
Chicken breast + rice noodles
+ soy sauce + broccoli,
mushrooms, pepper, onion

MEAT & POTATOES
Flank steak + red potatoes +
green beans

MAC & CHEESE
Elbow macaroni + milk + sharp
cheddar

GROWN-UP PBJ
Whole wheat bread + sliced
apple + almond butter

A YUMMY LOW-CAL BROWNIE ALTERNATIVE
Brownie mix + can of diet soda (no eggs, no oil)

SWEET TOOTH SATISFACTION
Nonfat yogurt +
granola + strawberry
halves + drop of
honey

OMELETTE
Eggs + leftover veggies + slice
of brea

CHIA SEED PUDDING
Coconut milk + ¼ cup chia
seeds + agave syrup

HOW TO NAVIGATE THE GROCERY STORE

We've all heard the "stick to the perimeter" rule when stocking up on groceries. But according to San Diego registered dietician Elizabeth Shaw, it's about balancing healthy items and the foods that'll satisfy your cravings.

- First things first: never shop on an empty stomach. You'll be more likely to make impulse purchases (try snacking on a banana before you shop).

- Go with a list. Make sure it hits on all the major food groups but also grab a few things that can satisfy a craving (one bakery donut, single-serving container of low-fat sorbet, dark chocolate pretzels, etc.).

- Hit the bread aisle and choose English muffins or tortillas, but choose ones that are high in fiber.

- The canned food aisle will have a great selection of beans (kidney, black, butter) and canned fruits. Grab some applesauce, it's a great snack and acts as a replacement for fat when baking.

- Hit the frozen food aisles for a mixed blend of veggies (they have the same nutrient density as fresh ones) and ground chicken or turkey for lean sources of protein.

- Stock up on in-season fruits and vegetables in your produce section. Shaw suggests grabbing potatoes if you're a French fry fan: slice them and bake them for a healthy alternative.

- Fat-free/low-fat dairy staples: plain yogurt, milk, and cheese—these should be in every gal's fridge.

- Don't be afraid to avoid the cereal aisle. If you love a sugary cereal, just make sure you portion it out.
- Other miscellaneous items to chuck in your cart? Peanut butter (check the shelves for PB2, it's nearly 1/4 the calories and fat of the regular version), condiments, low-sodium soy sauce, and individual serving bags to portion properly!

KEEP, TOSS, STORE

Unsure if something in the fridge has gone bad? When in doubt, use the smell test. Just don't ever taste something that might be past its prime.

That ancient pasta in your pantry? You can probably hang onto it. Unopened packages can last up to three years. If it's been opened, store the rest of it in an airtight container.

Mustard, mayo, ketchup— these are good for at least a month when refrigerated properly after use.

Don't wash fruit until it's ready to eat. Excess moisture will cause it to go bad faster.

A bottle of olive oil should be stored in a cool, dry place. Stick it in the fridge to extend its life even more —it can last up to two years (unless you're Italian like us and go through a bottle a month).

Cover already chopped up fruits and veggies in a sealable container. It'll help shelf life and make them easier to reuse.

Keep your coffee in the freezer—it'll last three weeks longer than if you stick it in the pantry.

Eat leftover cooked meat within three to four days. If it's still in the fridge past that time period, then chuck that beef chuck! Leftover cooked fish? Eat it within one or two days.

Spices and herbs last longer if stored in well-sealed containers. But salt? That puppy lasts indefinitely!

We don't know what's in a hot dog, but good news, an opened package lasts up to seven days. Let the BBQs begin!

The "sell by" date is not the same as the "use by" date. There's also the "best before" date. So many dates, so little time. The one to really stick to is the "use by" date—which should never be gobbled up if it's past its time. When you have doubts about fresh stuff, like meat from the butcher, ask the expert how long it'll last.

Not sure what to do with that deli meat drawer? Use it to stash items you actually use more regularly—don't keep it empty just because you don't have sliced ham on hand.

Love your frozen fruits and veggies? Stockpile them! Keep them organized by stuffing them into plastic file folders in your freezer.

We love bag caps. Stick them on any bags that go stale quickly—chips, cereal, you name it—in place of twist ties or using storage jars. They fit over bags and close tightly to keep your food fresher for longer. Search for them on amazon.com.

Depending on the make and model—the coldest part of the fridge varies. Keep items that need to be cool (vegetables, meat) wherever that spot is. (Look in your manual).

Want to know if that cinnamon you baked with a million years ago is still a go? Rub a bit in your hand, taste or smell it. If the aroma isn't obvious, it's lost its lust.

GET YOUR DRINK ON

H2O or bust. You should be drinking about nine cups of water a day— roughly 2.2 liters— according to the Mayo Clinic.

We love a hot cup of coffee in the morning. But too much can cause headaches and affect how you sleep. Experts say the recommended limit is around 300 mg, which means one 16 oz. is technically already over your limit. It's up to you to decide, but if your heart rate is pumping, stick to a small cup.

Cocktail time! Did you know the higher the alcohol content, the higher the calories? Thank goodness for Skinny Girl® margaritas.

A glass of wine a day can keep the doctor away: it can raise your good cholesterol and promote longevity overall. But just one glass a day—not a bottle.

Lots of women are advised to splurge on organic milk versus regular. The real benefit is the added omega-3 fatty acids, which are great for fighting heart disease. But either way, get your calcium.

Consider doing a cocktail/mocktail mash-up when you're out. If you've had one cosmo, order your next one without the booze to save on caloric intake.

When it comes to mixers: TOCs—your table of contents for a low-calorie drink are Tonic, Orange Juice, or Cranberry Juice.

Want to know the best teas for your health? Remember the colors: white, black, and green.

Unsure of what that cocktail you're having is gonna cost you calorie-wise? Check out getdrunknotfat.com.

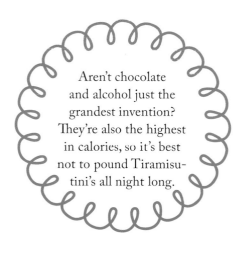

Aren't chocolate and alcohol just the grandest invention? They're also the highest in calories, so it's best not to pound Tiramisu-tini's all night long.

PAIR THIS WITH THAT

One rule of thumb when trying to match a drink with a meal—stick within the cultures. For example, a Mexican beer will always work with tacos and merlot is always tasty with pasta.

The meal: Beef or pork
The drink: A dry, red wine or a porter
Try: OneHope California Cabernet Sauvignon

The meal: Roast chicken or turkey
The drink: White wine
Try: Attems Pinot Grigio

The meal: A panini or fried chicken sandwich
The drink: Rose or a pale ale
Try: Nicolas Feuillatte Rose

The meal: Chocolate cake
The drink: Zinfandel or aged whiskey
Try: The Macallan

The meal: Pasta with red sauce
The drink: Chianti
Try: Ruffino Riserva Chianti Classico

The meal: Salmon
The drink: A Belgian-beer
Try: Allagash White

The meal: Risotto
The drink: Champagne
Try: Veuve Cliquot Brut Yellow Label

SO YOU WANNA BE A VEGETARIAN?

Ali Lopez, head chef of Omega FoodWorks in New York, cooks for vegetarians and vegans for a living. Thinking of changing your ways? Here are her easy ways to go meat-free.

1. Do your research. Read up on nutrition and learn about vitamins, minerals, protein, carbs, fat, iron, and what your daily needs are. There are healthy and unhealthy vegetarians.

2. Know your reasons. It might be moral or ethical regarding the treatment of animals, health reasons, environmental reasons, religious reasons, or a combination.

3. Start small. You don't have to give up meat "cold turkey" or all at once. Make the transition slowly, having more
vegetarian meals several times a week.

4. Learn to cook. It gives you the freedom to eat a more varied diet and gain a valuable skill. For vegetarians, it gives you the chance to avoid unhealthy options.

5. Read food labels. In addition to avoiding animal products, reading labels helps you become aware of what you are putting in your body. Try to use as many fresh, unprocessed foods as possible. And if you buy packaged foods, try and have the ingredient list as short as possible and that lists ingredients that you recognize and can pronounce.

6. Experiment. Try a new vegetable, fruit, or grain each week. Visit salad bars and farmers markets. There are a ton of great vegetarian cooking blogs and cookbooks for you to explore.

7. Eat clean, balanced meals and include one protein source at each meal. Don't just eat all carbs or load up on fruits and veggies. Add grains, nuts, seeds, and beans.

8. Eat at ethnic restaurants. Indian, Mexican, Asian, Mediterranean cuisines all offer many exciting and different vegetarian options.

9. Tell your friends and family. Not to try and convert them to your way of eating but to help them understand and support it.

10. Listen to your body. Vegetarian diets may not work for everybody, so pay attention to how it is affecting your health.

Real Chick Tip

Always keep a pitcher of ice water with lemon and lime in your refrigerator. It's great to have on hand in case a guest swings by.

Lauren, 27, NY, fundraiser

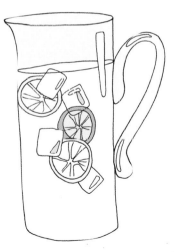

HEALTH & FITNESS

"I HEARD A DEFINITION ONCE: HAPPINESS IS HEALTH AND A SHORT MEMORY! I WISH I'D INVENTED IT, BECAUSE IT IS VERY TRUE."

—Audrey Hepburn

With a busy, on-the-go lifestyle filled with dating, school, work, and a million reasons to forgo a yoga power hour in lieu of happy hour, it's not uncommon for our health to plummet down the priority list. But we're here to tell you that it most definitely shouldn't—and in between all that other stuff we're dealing with, it's possible to do good things for our bodies and minds day in and day out, without sacrificing too much time or money. And if you wiggle in a healthy routine today, you'll have less to worry about in the future. Plus, good health equals lots of other good in your life, and who doesn't want a double dose of that?

WORK IT OUT, GIRL

Stretch every day right when you wake up to get your blood flowing. It's more beneficial than you think. If your dog or cat do it every time they wake up, it must be good for us, right? Here's a simple one: Lace your fingers together and lift your hands up over you head; hold for up to fifteen seconds and relax.

The treadmill can get tiring fast. If you find yourself losing steam, don't give up—just lower the speed to a pace you're more comfortable with and work up from there. You're not in a race.

Get your sneakers at a specialty store, where the salespeople have more knowledge about the products. If they ask you to run in store, don't be shy—they'll study your stride and match it with the perfect pair of shoes. Shop for them later in the day when your feet are at their biggest.

If you're the kind of person that quits workout routines easily, tell someone what your plan is before you start. Either work out with them or have them ask for updates on your progress. Feeling accountable will help keep you on track.

Prefer the evening? Toss them on first thing after work or class—even if you've got other things to do first.

No pain, no gain. Not necessarily. Whatever you're doing—yoga, running, weights—if something really hurts, stop what you're doing, especially if you find yourself wincing.

Try to do something for thirty minutes daily, at least four to five days a week. For example, instead of watching that rerun of *Friends,* power walk around the block. Or jump rope while you're watching Rachel and Ross break up, get together, repeat.

Write something motivational on your gym sneakers. Your wedding date, your goal weight—anything that will remind you each time you eye them in the closet.

Sign up for a 5k so you have something to work towards. Already a 5k-er? Try a 10k . . .

If you're a morning exerciser, put your workout clothes on as soon as you get out of bed—or better yet, fall asleep in them.

Whenever you plan to work out—but then cancel on your plan—put a buck in a "Regrets" jar. Getting fit *should* be expensive if that's what takes you to move. (Use that money later for a Zumba class or a post-workout smoothie).

Caught an illness of some sort? If what's got you down is all above your neck, it's probably okay to exercise—just take it easy. Otherwise, take the day off.

Get achy ankles when you run? Dirt paths are easier on your joints than pavement. Soak them in Epsom salt to get rid of pain post-run.

Gym memberships are often overpriced. Invest in dumbbells, a yoga mat, and exercise DVDs. Mix those at-home sessions with runs outside, and you'll see a difference in your physique and wallet.

Tape a pic of your former skinny self to the inside of the pantry, so you're forced to ask . . . Cheez-Its or chiseled stomach? Which do I prefer?

Crunches hurt your neck?
Press your tongue to the roof
of your mouth to help align
your noggin.

Forget about the number
on the scale and notice the
changes in your body with a
measuring tape.

Real Chick Tip

Vary your routine. I recently lost weight on Jenny Craig, but couldn't have lost as much as I did without working out. It seemed like such a daunting task at first, so I started out running, very slowly. But sometimes after a long day, I couldn't stomach the idea of getting on a treadmill. So I began to mix it up. I started taking spinning classes, then tried Zumba, Pilates, and hot yoga. Belly dancing is next on my list! When you're doing something new and exciting it doesn't feel like you're working out, so you're more likely to keep up your healthy routine!

–Lauren, 27, NY, office manager

FIVE STEPS TO FLAT ABS

The holy grail of a hot bod: a washboard stomach. To find out how to attain it, we enlisted the aide of health and fitness expert Jennifer Cohen, trainer on the CW's *Shedding for the Wedding*, president and CEO of NGR—No Gym Required—*and* a Weight Watchers spokesperson. Here's the deal:

1. **Don't just focus on one body part.** People often think that doing hundreds of crunches is the way to a flat belly, but it's just not so. It's way more effective to do a move like a push up where you're forced to engage your entire core region. This works all sections of the abdominals more effectively than a set of crunches. You burn more calories when you work more muscles at a time, which will help get you to your goal faster!

2. **Diet, diet, diet!** To get the abs you want, it's 85 percent what you do in the kitchen and 15 percent what you do at the gym. For your abs to show, you need to lose body fat and eat very clean. Keep a close eye on nutrition and calorie count.

3. **Keep up with your cardio.** It will help you burn body fat and show off your muscle work. Cardio with a good diet will help accelerate the process.

4. **Consistency is the key to success.** Anyone can stick to a plan for a day, but real results come from long-term commitment. It takes four weeks to replace a bad habit with a good one. Why not start today?

5. **Set small goals to encourage yourself along the way.** Pick non-food rewards to celebrate that progress. Treat yourself to a show, or go shopping. Non-food rewards will keep your spirits up without ruining your good habits.

YOU ARE WHAT YOU EAT . . .
YOU LITTLE SPICY TUNA ROLL, YOU

Drinking water throughout the day can help curb your appetite. Sipping on two glasses of water before a meal helps you fill up on liquid volume—so you end up eating less during the meal.

As soon as you feel hungry between meals, chew on a piece of strong, refreshing gum.

Real Chick Tip

"Pack your gym bag the night before and leave it right in front of your door. That way you can't forget it, so you won't 'forget' to go to the gym!"

−Susie, 23, NYC,
advertising account manager

Yogurts with live cultures or probiotics (just look on the label) are clutch for regulating your digestive system. Keep that in mind when you're feeling a little iffy in the tummy.

Frozen foods are a good way to practice portion control, but when you hit that aisle, look for options that have less than 300 calories and less than eight grams of fat.

When you look at a glass of soda, picture a glass of dirt—because you may as well be drinking that anyway. It does nothing for your body except wreck it. Switch to club soda or seltzer, which has the fizz you want without all the calories and sugar.

Anything you eat that's white, nix it from your diet—or at least limit it. Become a whole-grain girl. Bread, pasta, rice, bagels . . .

If the label says fat-free or low-fat, it may still be loaded with sugar, real or fake. Check the nutrition label rather than trust the packaging.

Don't be afraid to veer from what the recipe calls for. Does something call for butter? Substitute olive oil. A dessert that asks for extra sugar? Use applesauce.

Fruit is awesome—but not all fruit is created equal. Grapes, bananas, dried fruit and figs are super laden with sugar—no good. Instead, reach for raspberries, strawberries, apples, peaches, cantaloupes, or grapefruit.

If you're a late-night snacker, do something that keeps your hands busy right when you're about to eat. Polish your nails, pick up your Kindle, or slip your hands into a set of Paraffin gloves. Cravings last for about five minutes.

Use small plates so a small helping looks larger than it actually is.

Whenever you're about to snack but aren't even hungry, say it out loud: "I'm eating even though I'm not hungry." The number of times you say it daily may surprise you—and hopefully wake you up, embarrass you, or change your ways!

Out to din-din? Have the waiter put half of your entrée in a to-go bag and serve you the rest. Split a dessert, if your sweet tooth is rearing its head.

When in doubt (and itching for a nosh), frozen edamame rocks.

Need to eat more veggies? Whenever you serve a sit-down dinner, bring the bowl of good stuff (salad, roasted peppers, whatever you made) to the table, and leave the meat, rice and so on over on the stovetop. You'll snack more on what's right in front of you.

A clean plate isn't always a "good job" anymore. Try to leave the last three bites at all your meals to instantly cut a good number of calories from your daily intake.

WHITTLE WHILE YOU WORK

The office, the library . . .
wherever you spend your days,
park as far away from the
entrance as possible.

When Mother Nature calls,
take the stairs to a restroom
on another floor.

Really want to tone up? Swap your office
chair to an exercise ball. One study
showed that sitting on one of those guys
burns nearly six percent more calories
than when you work on a typical chair.

"IT'S NOT ABOUT PERFECT. IT'S ABOUT
EFFORT. AND WHEN YOU BRING THAT
EFFORT EVERY SINGLE DAY, THAT'S
WHERE TRANSFORMATION HAPPENS.
THAT'S HOW CHANGE OCCURS."
—JILLIAN MICHAELS

Use the stairs. If you're on the 97th floor, start slow and take the elevator the rest of the way up. When you're ready, tack on another ten flights and so on.

Take a break from your computer screen for at least fifteen minutes every two hours to walk around inside or catch some fresh air.

Print your docs to a machine across the room—not right next to your cube.

Start a Wednesday salad club with a few other health-conscious coworkers. Here's what you do: Each week, assign a category to each member. Say you bring veggies one week, someone else takes fruit, another handles protein, another the lettuce and so on. In the end, you'll only have to bring one ingredient (enough for everyone), but get to enjoy a full, nutritious salad.

ARE YOU GETTING ENOUGH NUTRIENTS, YOUNG LADY?

Dr. Melina Jampolis is a Cali-based internist and board-certified physician nutrition specialist with a focus on nutrition for weight loss and disease prevention and treatment (bet you've seen her on *Dr. Oz* or *Live with Regis and Kelly*), and for our handy guidebook, she narrowed in on some key nutrients that many women in their twenties might not be getting enough of—along with tips for how to incorporate them on a regular basis.

WHAT YOU NEED	WHY YOU NEED IT	WHERE TO GET IT
Calcium and Vitamin D	Your bone mass is near its peak by the age of 20, but it can continue building until you hit 30, so getting plenty of these important bone builders during your 20s is essential. Your daily calcium goal should be 1000mg, the amount in about 3 servings of dairy a day, and 600 IU of vitamin D.	You can also get plenty of calcium from non-dairy sources including calcium-fortified soy milk and juice, tofu, soybeans, soynuts, bok choy, broccoli, collard greens, kale, and mustard greens. Vitamin D is tough to get from your diet unless you eat vitamin D fortified foods, but UVB rays from the sun help your skin produce it. Unfortunately, sunscreen with an SPF of eight or more (which you should definitely be wearing in your twenties to protect your skin) blocks UVB rays, so you might want to consider taking a vitamin D supplement along with calcium if you aren't getting enough from your diet.

WHAT YOU NEED	WHY YOU NEED IT	WHERE TO GET IT
Iron	The blood you lose during your monthly period can deplete your body's iron stores. If you don't eat red meat often, are a serious athlete, or have very heavy periods, you have to make sure that your iron levels don't drop too low, which can lead to anemia and fatigue.	Consider taking a multivitamin with iron (the RDA for women in their twenties is 18mg). You can also get iron from plant-based foods like spinach, dried fruit, dried beans, and whole grains, but this type of iron is not absorbed as well unless you combine it with vitamin C rich foods like citrus, tomatoes, or tomato sauce.
Folic Acid	This B vitamin is critical for women of child-bearing age. Low levels can lead to severe birth defects in babies.	Leafy greens, fruits, dried beans, peas, and enriched breads and cereals are good sources, but the easiest way to ensure that you get your daily dose is to take a multivitamin with 400 mcg per day. If you are taking birth control pills, a multivitamin containing all the B vitamins may be especially important as research shows that the pill can lower blood levels of vitamin B6—which is important for protein metabolism and also helps produce mood and energy boosting chemicals in your brain.

WHAT YOU NEED	WHY YOU NEED IT	WHERE TO GET IT
Omega 3 Fatty Acids (DHA & EPA)	These essential fatty acids (they are essential to eat because your body can't produce them) are very important to help women in their twenties look and feel great. They can help protect your heart and brain, decrease your risk of depression, and keep your skin looking radiant.	You can get what you need from two servings per week of fatty fish like salmon, tuna, trout, sardines, and mackerel, or you can take a daily omega 3 fatty acid fish oil supplement (500 mg) if fish isn't your thing. If you take birth control pills, which can increase your risk of blood clots, omega 3 fatty acids may be especially beneficial as they can help prevent blood clots. Flaxseeds, walnuts, and chia seeds are also super healthy, but they do not have the same health benefits as fish.
Probiotics	These "friendly" bacteria have been linked with loads of health promoting benefits including keeping you regular (something you might need if your on-the-go lifestyle involves a bit too much fast food, packaged food or alcohol), supporting your immune system, and even keeping your 'lady parts' healthy.	You can get probiotics from fortified foods including yogurt and even chocolate bars, or from dietary supplements. Different probiotics have different functions, so you may have to do a little homework to figure out which one will work best for you. Fermented foods like kefir, non-fortified yogurt, sauerkraut, and kim chee, also contain healthful, friendly bacteria but they don't have specific health effects.

BE WELL

Toothache? Suck on a cough drop. Works like magic.

Get a Pap smear. Every. Single. Year. The National Cancer Institute decrees that most cancers of the cervix can be prevented if you get regular Paps, and can be treated better if caught early, too.

Before each appointment, write down any questions or concerns on a notepad and bring it with you. Nothing worse than leaving without remembering to bring something up.

If your Pap comes back abnormal, don't panic. They're super sensitive and can often pick up the slightest change in your cervix. Ask your doc if you should return in six months or sooner.

When you're slathering on the sunscreen, picture a shot glass. That's how much is recommended to use to cover your entire body. Oh—and wear sunscreen in the winter, too.

Research done at Rutgers showed that flowers are good for your emotional health, triggering happy emotions when they're around. Buy yourself a bouquet or tell your significant other why he should get 'em for you—often.

Those forms you're asked to fill out at the doc's office shouldn't be taken lightly. Ask your parents about your family's medical history, then relay that to the doctor.

Sleep actually affects weight loss. You need your zzz's in order to get your body working properly and in tip-top shape. If you can't hit the hay easily, try this: take a warm bath with a few drops of essential oils thirty minutes before bed to get relaxed. And never bring your work between the sheets—keeping your bed a snooze sanctuary is crucial to counting sheep.

Daily brain games can help stave off dementia and Alzheimer's in the long run, so do a crossword before you sleep or even take the time to meditate. Same thing goes for using your less dominant hand for tasks, like handling chopsticks or brushing your teeth.

When you gotta go, don't hold it—no matter how inconvenienced you may feel. Stagnant urine can cause UTIs. And always pee after sex—that helps cut down on them, too.

Also, wash your hands *before* and after to zap germs you've collected on your hands prior to your pit stop.

If you're ever in an emergency that requires calling 9-1-1, state your exact location before anything else so help can be dispatched right away.

Real Chick Tip

If you are having a bad day, get outside. The sun will instantly make you feel better.

–Dana, 24, NY,
social worker

SELF-DEFENSE IN A NUTSHELL

Whenever you ride in an elevator, stand near the buttons—not cornered in the back.

If work or any of your to-dos requires you going to a sketchy part of town, tell someone first where you're headed.

Have your keys in hand when you walk to your car—not buried in the abyss of your Furla bag.

Walking outside, alone? Don't talk on the cell. Predators know you'll be distracted and won't hear anyone coming. You may think it's better—you can tell your pal you're in trouble, right?—but by the time the person on the other end of the phone gets help, it could be too late.

If someone calls and asks for your roommate—but he or she is out—don't admit that. Say they're unable to get to the phone, but you can take a message.

Sleep with your keys next to your bed. If you hear a break-in, activate your car's alarm to get attention and scare them off.

Running with headphones? Leave one earbud in, one out.

Keep a whistle on your keychain in case you need help or you spot someone else that needs attention.

Someone shady show up at your front door? Rather than opening it, yell out that you're hosting friends, but that they can leave a business card in your mailbox.

Late night at the mall and the parking lot is looking foreboding? Ask a police officer or security guard to escort you to the car.

Be aware of your surroundings. If you look confident and keep your head on a swivel you'll make yourself less appealing to a potential attacker. If you feel like someone is following you, don't be afraid to look them in the eyes. Now they know you can identify them.

If you know you're about to be attacked, look around for anything that can be used as a weapon—a baseball bat, your umbrella, a wine bottle, kitchen knives . . .

We could go on and on with self-defense tips, but the best way to be prepared is to take an actual self-defense class. Find one in your area and enroll yourself and a few friends.

SCARY SITUATIONS

When she's not kicking ass in class or working with celebs like Bethenny Frankel, Gabrielle Rubin—founder of and instructor at Female Awareness Self-Defense in New York City—is educating ladies like us on how to stay safe. We asked her about three scenarios. Here's what she said to do if . . .

YOU'RE BEING FOLLOWED . . .

If you're not sure whether you're being followed, go ahead and turn around. Look past the guy and sway left and right, as if you're waiting for someone who's late. You could even wave; chances are your follower won't turn around to see who you're waving at. Definitely have someone on your trail? Take off running, but act out a reason for it, such as looking at your watch and indicating you're late or answering a pretend emergency call from someone. Then cross the street. Go into a store, restaurant, anywhere populated. Call for a ride outta there.

YOU'RE BEING MUGGED . . .

Usually, muggers don't have their hands on you; they just want your items. Always remember this: those things can be replaced, you can't be. Throw your wallet—or whatever he asks for—to the ground past him. (If you hand it over, you risk him getting control of your wrist. Never get close enough so he can grab you.) As soon as he bends down to pick up the item, that's your cue to take off running.

YOU'RE BEING ATTACKED . . .

If he's behind you, kick your heel up from your knee so you can hit his shin, knee, or groin. If he's in front of you, bring your knee up and slam your heel down on his foot. Use your body parts as a weapon—scratch his face, poke his eyes, anything to avert his attention so you can get away. And through it all, don't forget to scream. "Fire" will get others' attention and hopefully some help.

HEARTBREAK

"ONLY TIME CAN HEAL YOUR BROKEN HEART.
JUST AS ONLY TIME CAN HEAL HIS BROKEN
ARMS AND LEGS."

—*Miss Piggy*

Headaches, the flu, the occasional UTI—
these pesky physical problems are often solved
with a quick call to the pharmacy. You can't,
however, take the excruciating pain out of a
broken heart with a simple antidote. Even if
you're the one doing the dumping, it's still
a dirty and heart-wrenching deed. What's a
love-scorned girl to do? First, take comfort
in knowing that everyone has gone through
this. And you know what? They survived and
so will you. Sit back, relax and pour yourself a glass of
wine. We've collected the best advice on how to sail safely past
your messy wreckage to a stronger and happier you.

Write down everything you hated about
your ex: an inability to say thanks, a beer
gut, the way they droned on and on about
work but never asked about yours, then read
it out loud. You'll feel instantly better.

Download the iPhone app
called "Daily Affirmations" for
99 cents. Open it whenever you
need a strength booster.

Cry it out. Break a dish. Punch the sofa cushion. Hold a pillow up to your face and scream as loud as you can.

Start referring to him or her as "the Ex." The less you use a name, the sooner they'll become just another old memory.

Let this pity party last for a few days, then give yourself a good look in the mirror: this is not the best version of you. And why the hell would you continue allowing that to happen?

Delete their phone number. Why would you give yourself the opening to place a drunk dial? That never leads to *anything* good.

Don't force answers. It's possible you may never know why you've been dumped. Instead focus on what went right in the relationship, and what you learned for next time. It's pointless to fixate on what you *think* you did wrong.

Throw out the left-behind stuff—and all the stuff that reminds you of your ex. Cards, stuffed animals, the sexy lingerie you wore, and, yes, all those photos from around the Caribbean of the two of you.

. . . But hang on to the valuable stuff, like the jewelry from Christmas. Those baubles can make a pretty penny online.

Don't beg him or her to come back. If your break-up isn't meant to be permanent, it won't be.

Okay so maybe we're being harsh. If you must save something sentimental, hide it under your bed in a shoebox until you're certain you can look at it without blubbering.

If someone says one of the following: I'm not good enough for you, it's not you it's me—believe them.

"DON'T CRY FOR THE MAN WHO'S LEFT YOU—THE NEXT ONE MAY FALL FOR YOUR SMILE."
—MAE WEST

Turn off the radio. Every song will remind you of your failed relationship.

Ugh, Facebook. Why must you torture us? If you can't stand seeing your ex's updates in your News Feed, "unsubscribe" from them. Or simply unfriend them altogether.

No matter how much you loved the ex's family and vice versa, they get lost in the divorce. It's for the best.

Start something new that will get your angst out—a hip-hop dancing class, karate, or kickboxing. You'll get the stress out and slim down as your new single self.

But don't bring a random home to find some solace. You don't need to wake up with any added pains.

Volunteer for something as a reminder that you are a good gal with a lot going on. Type in your ZIP code at volunteermatch.org.

When you're out, make eye contact with those you find attractive. The flirty feeling that transmits during those intimate, fleeting moments will slowly charge you up to the idea of being with someone new.

DVR episodes of *Ellen* for laughter, and watch her before you go to bed. No crying yourself to sleep tonight!

Call your parents. Mom and Dad have had so much more experience than you. There's nothing more soothing than pops calling you his little princess when you're pushing thirty.

Watch *The First Wives Club* for strength. Over and over again. *"You don't own me. . . ."*

Say yes to every social invitation you get for two weeks straight. Sitting on the couch won't actually make you feel better, but being around people will.

Cut off all communication with your Ex. Out of sight, out of mind. Don't you dare tell yourself that you "value the friendship" when you want to call him.

Three words: Girls. Night. Out. Throw on some skimpy clothes, hit the bar, toss back a few drinks, and start up a game of Truth or Dare.

Embrace the sexual freedom that comes with your single life. Start a free blog about it at onsugar.com (anonymously of course), or keep a diary of your new sexual conquests.

Refresh your abode so it's not the same stale place. Rearrange furniture, paint a wall and buy a few new trinkets.

Book a spa appointment with your closest friends. A new look, a new you!

YOU'VE BEEN DUMPED

BURN THIS

No, not the ex's clothes. This kick-ass, get-over-it-now CD playlist.

1. I'm Gone, I'm Going—Lesley Roy

2. The King of Wishful Thinking—Ace and Kings

3. Fighter—Christina Aguilera

4. Lonely—Britney Spears

5. Makes Me Wonder—Maroon 5

6. Goodbye—Kristina DeBarge

7. Starting Now—Ingrid Michaelson

8. Tears Dry On Their Own—Amy Winehouse

9. Are You Happy Now?—Michelle Branch

10. He Wasn't Man Enough—Toni Braxton

11. Move Along—The All-American Rejects

12. Goodbye Earl—Dixie Chicks

DEALING WITH REJECTION

Take it from Kimberley Kennedy—author of the bestselling memoir, *Left at the Altar*—rejection is not the end of the world. Here, she dishes to us her expert, firsthand advice on overcoming the big R.

- **Don't let the rejection define you.** Despite how you feel now, you are NOT unlovable, worthless, or incapable of ever finding love again. Just because you weren't a good fit for them, doesn't mean you won't be the perfect fit for someone else.

- **Reject your failed relationship, not yourself.** Any time a happy memory enters your mind, immediately replace it with a negative one. This is a deliberate act that will be hard at first, but it's critical to healing. Focus on the reality, not the fantasy.

- **Don't encourage more rejection.** If your ex made the uncomfortable decision to move on, they likely mean it. Devising ways to make him change his mind probably won't work and could only make you feel worse.

- **Allow yourself to be happy.** Be mindful that too much mourning can turn to self-pity. Your family and friends will be sympathetic to mourning—self-pity, not so much.

YOU DID THE DUMPING

Give yourself time to think about why things aren't working out. You should be completely prepared and ready to do it before you actually do it.

Be gentle (if it is deserved). Think about how you would want to be dumped.

Real Chick Tip

Turn to your support group. Everything I lost when I had my heart broken was found in my amazing friends and family. It became clear who I could really trust and rely on when I needed to be picked up off the ground.

−Meghan, 26, Chicago, graduate student

Be ready for any attempts to sway you back and know what you're going to say in advance. Practice on a girlfriend beforehand.

When you're actually pulling the plug, remain a classy lady. Listen to their rebuttals, say goodbye, and continue on your way.

Be careful about the friends zone. Mention that you hope to be friends in the future, and stop at that. If you guys get chummy now, it's a slippery slope into becoming friends with benefits, which never ends well.

Don't be a coward. No texting, phone calls, emails, or Post-It notes. Face-to-face is the right way to go.

Don't use someone because you're lonely. Booty calling or just dialing up for a pick-me-up is unfair to them and to you.

Enjoy being single. You asked for it, so make the most of it! Pull on those heels, grab your girlfriends, and flirt with someone—as soon as you feel ready.

This is going to sound awful, but dress up for the break-up talk. You'll feel more confident and will be less likely to back out.

For every day you stall, that's another day to tack on to your history together, making it harder to split. Rip the bandage off as soon as you know it's over.

Your ex has been dishing the dirt to mutual friends? Don't stoop to that level. Tell them that what they've heard is just one side of the story and that you think the details should remain private.

Let your ex get over you. If you hear about them moving on, don't let that tinge of jealousy make you reach out.

If he or she didn't necessarily "deserve" the breakup (no cheating, no backstabbing, etc.), avoid posting pics of you and a new love right away on Facebook without fair warning. It's the nice thing to do.

If you decide to defriend on Facebook, check your privacy settings. Make sure your wall, status, or photos can't be seen.

Familiar with this sticky situation? You love the friends, but not your ex. If you keep in touch with them, do so in ways that won't upset any one (via email or phone.) Don't go to their parties (at least for awhile) or invite them to yours. If you do continue the friendships, keep the intimate details of your relationship and breakup to yourself. It's between the two of you. That's all.

WEDDING WOES

Calling off your big day—no matter how far along in the process you are—can be the hardest thing you've done in your life yet. Kathy Dawson, Cleveland relationship coach and author of *Diagnosis: Married—How to Deal with Marital Conflict, Heal Your Relationship, and Create a Rewarding and Fulfilling Marriage* told us the tips she shares with her clients:

- **Step back from party planning and focus on your relationship at hand.** Are you fighting all the time? Is it taking away from the fun of it all?

- **Remember: you're not the first person to do this.** Women before you have pulled the plug on the whole operation. You're allowed to break it off, or simply postpone it.

- **Put it into perspective.** Think losing the cash you put in so far is bad? Guess how much a divorce can be . . .

- **Just get it over with.** Sit down with your parents and talk about the best way to go about this. It's not easy, but it takes courage, and you've got it.

Real Chick Tip

Recall the times you've survived in the past. I can remember a bunch of occasions when I swore that a certain fellow was "the one." Every time, I swore that was it. In my mind, the world was ending and I would never have feelings for anyone else ever again. I am happy to say that I've proved myself wrong time and time again. Each time I eventually picked my heart up off the floor, dusted it off, and moved the hell on with a little more knowledge to take into my next relationship. I'm not saying it's easy. There has been ice cream and bad dates and a lot of other silly things in between. But in every case it's been the same. That feeling that I had been punched in the chest goes away. One day the sadness, the anger, or whatever other feeling I was holding onto would disappear. Trust me. There is little better than waking up and realizing your heart isn't broken anymore and starting your own story, fresh from page one.

—Margaret, 29, NYC, writer

IF YOU THINK YOU WANT SOMEONE BACK

Smell something of theirs. Studies have shown that smell can play a huge role in revealing your feelings. If the smell of your ex's shirt makes you feel warm and fuzzy, you may still have love there. If you get angry or it doesn't faze you, you're over it.

Don't become a booty call. Anyone that gets back with their ex strictly for sex, regrets it.

If patching things up is a go, proceed with caution. Don't just jump back into things and start where you left off. Go on a few dates and don't kiss. Ease back into it to see if it all makes sense.

If you approach your ex with the idea of getting back together and you discover they've already moved on, let it be. You'll find someone else, too.

Stop asking everyone's opinion because everyone will have one. Stick to your gut and your heart and go with it.

There will be moments where you'll wonder if you should offer a second chance. (Third chances are a huge no-no.) Force yourself to be honest. Are you just lonely or do you really miss this person? Remind yourself why you split up and question if the reasons are forgivable.

Before you jump back in bed, get the truth about whether or not they've been celibate since your breakup. This isn't so you can start a fight; it's for your health.

Don't smother each other with affection. Masking the problems you're trying to solve won't help in the long run.

Don't constantly bring up the past. If you've made the effort to move forward, do that.

Have a back-up plan. Agree on how to end things a second time if you realize it isn't working anymore so no one gets surprised.

Stick to your guns. Are you working towards a relationship under certain conditions? Take note of the changes and if he is taking them seriously.

IF THE JERK CHEATED ON YOU

Your ex may try to talk you into taking them back. If a person sounds like they've changed without you around, it's because they have. They've lost your physical and emotional support, and it might be more about missing a companion than it is about you.

Believe in karma. We'd bet a million bucks that every single person that has ever cheated has regretted the decision at one time or another.

Do not exact revenge. Don't even consider stooping to such a low level. Relationships are sacred and if you were with someone that did not consider this, it's better that they're gone.

No matter what he or she says about their level of intimacy while you two were dating, hit the gyno's office and get checked.

Don't check their Facebook, emails, or voice mails. Cut yourself off. You may think you want to know all, but you don't. Finding out the truth isn't going to be closure. It will prevent you from getting past the hurt.

"I LOVE TO SHOP AFTER A BAD RELATIONSHIP.
I DON'T KNOW. I BUY A NEW OUTFIT AND IT
MAKES ME FEEL BETTER. IT JUST DOES."
—RITA RUDNER

While you don't want to know more about
the homewrecker, you do want to know if
it's someone you know. Ask only that and
if it is a familiar face, ignore them.

Once a cheater, (most likely)
always a cheater. Sometimes
people make mistakes.
Sometimes they're just d-bags.
And sometimes you need to
go with your gut on this one.
Does this person strike you as a
repeat offender?

Don't blast your anger
on Facebook with a sad
breakup quote. Keep it
private. Word will get out.
Quell the inner psycho and
be the bigger person.

It's not about the other woman. Though
your natural reaction is to blame the
other lady involved, it isn't her fault.
You won't ever know what your ex
was actually telling her.

KNOCK THEM OFF THE PEDESTAL

Jamie Beckman, author of *The Frisky 30-Day Breakup Guide,* shares five ways to lower your opinion of your ex—just a tad!—to remind yourself that they might not be the rock star you thought.

1. **Think of the one thing that you always worried about when introducing your ex to someone.** Were they painfully antisocial or willfully dismissive of others? Did they refuse to shake hands or not bother to remember names or faces? Because if you internally cringe and hope that an introduction goes smoothly, there's probably something wrong. More specifically, something wrong with them.

2. **Hate on their fighting style.** There's a right way to handle tiffs and a wrong way, and now that you've broken up, I'm guessing you fought together the wrong way. Were your concerns ignored? Were you dismissed and called dramatic? Was there lots of yelling? Remember those times.

3. **Replay a bad moment.** Every relationship has that one oh-no-you-didn't moment, when someone says something so friggin' insensitive that you visibly shake with anger. Close your eyes. Recreate that scene in your head. Make yourself feel that way again, as much as it kills you to do so. Now open your eyes. Guess what? You're not in that situation anymore. Now you're free to find someone who would sooner impale themselves on a rusty sword than say anything like that to you.

4. **Realize they sucked the fun out of life; now put it back.** Women tend to trade in a good portion of their lives when they're in a relationship. What did you give up when you

were in your relationship with ol' what's-his-name? Now's the time for you to get all of that back and more—and next time around, if someone new makes fun of your constant need to listen to late-'90s folk singer-songwriters, you'll tell them exactly where to stick the attitude.

5. **Pinpoint a main flaw.** If we learned one thing in high school English class, it's that every character has a flaw. What was your ex's? Think of the one thing that you always hated. Bring it to the light. You will never have to deal with that ever again.

Real Chick Tip

Relish what doors their mistake opens for you. The best part about my boyfriend leaving me for his best friend's girlfriend was all the amazing sex I had with his best friend.

—Anonymous,
for very obvious reasons

SWEET, SWEET REVENGE

While we don't condone violence, vandalism, or public thrashing of your ex on all your major social media platforms, a little justice won't kill them. I mean, your ex can't just get off unscathed, right? Take your pick, ladies!

Change their e-mail's auto-response message to something embarrassing. Perhaps: "I'm currently out of the office, recovering from scabies."

Oopsy, daisy! Slip your hot pink thong in the wash with all their whites.

The old toothbrush trick. Clean the bathroom floor, the toilet, and the shower door—all with their trusty brusher. Then put it right back where you found it.

"GORGEOUS HAIR IS THE BEST REVENGE."
—IVANKA TRUMP

Get payback, literally. According to Essence.com, if you live in Hawaii, Illinois, Mississippi, New Mexico, North Carolina, South Carolina, or Utah, you can sue a mistress for "alienation of affection"—and make her pay for it.

Donate their Xbox to charity, then have the organization send a thank you email. What an angel!

HOUSEKEEPING

"I'M AN EXCELLENT HOUSEKEEPER. EVERY TIME
I GET A DIVORCE, I KEEP THE HOUSE."

—*Zsa Zsa Gabor*

While you can't always control the chaos in the real world, you can manage the inside of your own humble abode. The following tips work wherever you squat—and most of them require resources you already have on hand. We've also enlisted the pros for easy decorating ideas, suggestions for corralling an unruly closet, and the essential cleaners for every tedious task. Here's our golden rule of housekeeping: make sure you clean and organize on a regular basis. A hostess with the mostess always keeps a shipshape space for her guests, but even more importantly, coming home to a neat place can be a huge de-stressor for you. Even if you may not appreciate a clean house, your friends, one-night-stands, significant others, and Mom will. Mop to it!

ALL ABOUT YOUR HOME

Does your garbage reek? To absorb odors, leave a couple sheets of fabric softener sheets or newspaper in the bottom of the trashcan.

Nix bacteria from the refrigerator handle regularly by wiping it down with a disinfectant.

Pick up crumbs inside cabinets with your vacuum attachment or a damp cloth.

Deodorizing the dishwasher is a cinch. Fill a cup with white vinegar and place on the top rack. Run the washer to stop the stench.

Keep an open box of baking soda in your fridge to zap smells.

Son of a bitch! Someone spilled red wine on your pristine carpet? Oust the stain with a few drops of white wine. Or be a gracious hostess and proclaim; "Now when I see this spot I'll always remember this night!"

Spray the shower and tub with an all-purpose cleaner. We like Method's Tub & Tile (drugstore.com, $5.49).

Make cleaning the shower doors easy with a squeegee. Wipe the walls down after each shower.

Toss two dissolving antacid tables (pull the Alka-Seltzer from your hangover stash) into the toilet and let sit for fifteen to twenty minutes, then brush to clean.

Lift your baño ban and hit super dirty tubs with some liquid laundry detergent mixed with water.

Got unexpected guests arriving in ten minutes? If you clean one thing before they get there, make it the bathroom. It's the only place where people go solo and have a few seconds to notice how clean you are.

Tape a "no snooping" sign in your medicine cabinet to snub nosy guests.

Shine up mirrors using old newspapers instead of paper towels. They don't leave streaks.

Indoor plants—gotta love 'em. No TLC necessary, except when they get dusty. Bring small plants to the kitchen sink, and larger ones to the shower for a quick rinse.

Keep this in mind the next time you load your dishwasher— make plates face the center for a better clean job.

Freshen up curtains in the dryer along with a fabric softener sheet or a damp bath towel.

The only thing grosser than cleaning out a garbage disposal is the smell it can produce. Drop a lemon or lime peel down the hatch and run some hot water. You won't have to plug your nose any longer.

"EXCUSE THE MESS, BUT WE LIVE HERE."
—ROSEANNE BARR

Hair spray spots on the mirror? Use a little rubbing alcohol on a soft cloth.

Tipsy guest break a wine glass? Pick up shattered shards safely with rubber gloves and masking tape. Or try a slice of bread.

Clean the bottom of your iron by putting some salt on the ironing board, then press down and make the motions of an iron (just don't turn it on).

Use the brush attachment of a vacuum cleaner to tackle your blinds.

Keep a couple of old socks in your cleaning arsenal. If you notice things starting to look dusty, put one over your hand and wipe down all the surfaces in your place. Toss it in the hamper and reuse next time.

Remove perspiration stains on clothing by soaking in vinegar and warm water.

Next time you spill nail polish on your wood floor or furniture, let it dry—then scrape it off with a credit card or butter knife.

Remove tarnish from sterling silver with a dab of toothpaste and warm water.

Keep a basket of bathroom cleaning supplies in each bathroom. You'll be able to clean at a moment's notice if you hear guests arrive while you're popping a squat.

No time? Look—if you're really behind and can spare some bucks, go ahead and find a cleaner to handle your place. Enter your ZIP code at maids.com to find a reputable service near you.

Do a quick clean once a week and a big clean every other Saturday. Your apartment will stay cleaner if you don't avoid it all together.

Avoid heavily scented sprays or potpourri. It's a dated way to get your pad smelling good. Instead, use a reed diffuser or a soy candle. We like sweetgrassonline.com.

Always fill up a pot or pan with water when they go into the sink. If you slack off and leave them overnight, they'll be easier to clean if they've been soaking.

THE TWENTYSOMETHING'S HOUSECLEANING TOOLBOX

Debra Johnson, Training Manager of Merry Maids, says these are the cleaning essentials for every twentysomething girl.

Micro fiber cloths—attracts and holds dust rather than spreading dust around. Buy different color cloths for different tasks to avoid cross contamination.

Vacuum with attachments—allows flexibility to accomplish different detailed tasks.

Brushes—scrub brush, grout brush, and toilet brush will tackle any nook or cranny.

Micro fiber mop—choose one with a removable micro fiber head to toss into the washer after each use.

Timer—keep motivated by setting a timer for 5, 15, or 30 minutes to a task.

Must-have cleaning products—multi-purpose cleaner, degreaser, bathroom cleaner for soap scum, and a floor cleaner.

Floor steamer—All you need is water to make all your floors sparkle and shine.

ALL ABOUT YOUR PERSONAL STUFF

Stubborn price tags on your new purchase can easily be removed with a Q-tip soaked with rubbing alcohol.

Deodorant stains are the worst! Sponge them off with a microfiber cloth.

Real Chick Tip

Live alone at least once. After I broke up with my boyfriend, I got my own apartment. I didn't know I had to turn on electricity and lived with an extension cord out of my door and plugged into a hallway outlet, so I didn't have to shower in the dark. That's just one thing you learn when you live alone. Learn to take care of yourself, by yourself, with no one's help. Once you've done that, you can survive anything.

–Hillary, 27, CT, HR specialist

Are your white camisole, sheets, and undies looking a bit yellow? Soak overnight in a bucket filled with water and one cup of lemon juice.

Freshen up a sticky curling iron by rubbing it with a cotton pad dampened in rubbing alcohol. Make sure it's off first!

Got a CD of music or data that's sporting a not-so-welcomed scratch? Buff it with a cotton pad dabbed with toothpaste, and then rinse with water.

Please, please wash your bed sheets at least every other week. Not once a month. Think of all the sweat and fluids you're probably dozing in.

Clean up makeup brushes by running water over the bristles, then adding a drop of shampoo. Lather and rinse, then use a towel to squeeze out extra water. After they air dry, they'll feel like new.

Vintage or out-of-season clothes come bearing musty, stale odors. Kill the stench by spritzing the duds with a little bit of vodka. No, they won't smell like Sunday's morning walk of shame. Vodka is odorless and fab at eradicating bacteria.

A dash of baking soda and hot water are clutch at cleaning hairbrushes and combs.

For wrinkles between buttons on your blouse, use your straightening iron.

Perk up a limp . . . floral arrangement! Fill the vase with water and drop in two Alka-Seltzer tablets.

Get blood out (um, cw) of fabrics (i.e. period pantics) with hydrogen peroxide. Apply it to the stain then wash as usual.

Before you put your winter clothes into hibernation during the summer (or vice versa), clean them. It may sound like a waste of time, but moths are drawn to stains.

We're not going to tell you to make your bed every day, because we know you won't. But at least make it when you have guests. You never know when they'll ask for a tour of your pad.

Keep a fancy bar of soap in your underwear drawer. Why? They'll smell sexy all the time—which could come in handy one night. You can thank us later.

Real Chick Tip

Have open conversations with your room-mates about how you like to live. I was living with a girl and sharing one bathroom, and because she was kind of a tomboy, I never thought much of the fact that she didn't keep many products in there. Not even a loofah. Well, I got home one day and saw my loofah in the trash. I asked her why, and she said that she bought us a new one. Needless to say, we had a lengthy talk about personal hygiene fairly immediately. I asked her to move out about six weeks later.

–Jessica B., 27, Australia, publicist

THE ULTIMATE WARDROBE MALFUNCTION

Dayna Bradoff, the twentysomething owner of organizing company Chaos Theory NYC, weighs in on battling a closet that is bursting at the seams.

- Go through all your clothing from the season that has just passed—if there's anything that you haven't worn, it's time to let it go. Donate! Host a clothing swap. Or sell your goods (see Chapter 11, MONEY).

- Rotate out-of-season clothes and accessories. If you're short on space, check with local dry cleaners—many of them offer boxed sweater storage so you can clear the decks for things you'll actually wear this spring and summer.

- Try on your clothes. If something doesn't fit, add it to the toss out pile. Make a list of items you need to add to your wardrobe, too—shopping is way more fun than cleaning.

- Velvet hangers keep even the skinniest spaghetti strap for slipping.

- Closet shelves can be great for stacking folded items; keep those piles upright by using shelf dividers.

- Use the inside of your closet to display your jewelry collection. Hang a simple bulletin board and use tacks as pegs for your necklaces and bracelets, for a tangle-free solution.

Spritz a bit of your perfume into the dryer before you turn it on. Your clothes will come out with a whiff of your signature scent.

Did you shrink your favorite sweater? Sorry, can't help you with that. But at least crop tops are in again. Hurray!

DECORATING ON A DIME

Don't feel rushed to have a decorated apartment. If you try and decorate all at once, you'll be broke and eventually regret half of your purchases.

Never underestimate the power of hooks. Use them in the bathroom, in your closet and behind doors so there's never an excuse to toss things on the floor.

Check out a local wallpaper supplier and buy old books or discontinued rolls. Use them on the back of bookshelves, on one wall of the bathroom or in your closet for surprise pops of design.

Make a "décor to do" list. Want a big mirror above your couch? A new headboard? Check off one thing at a time and stick to a budget.

Frame your personal documents for one-of-a-kind artwork. Flaunt that D+ paper or your very first parking ticket to be a little tongue in cheek, or a note one of your best friends passed to you in the fifth grade for sentimental value.

Buy vases in bulk from discount craft suppliers (try save-on-crafts.com) and use them as a traveling vignette in your apartment. They look great grouped together for a dinner party or separated in every corner of the house.

For an instant entry, hang a vintage mailbox, lay down a doormat, and place a stool or seat against the wall. It's an instant way to corral bills, keys and shoes.

Don't buy new. You may have your very first adult apartment, but don't feel like it needs to be decked out in Pottery Barn. Check out flea markets, consignment shops, and Goodwill.

Shop at Grandma's. Vintage linens, embroidered art, and teapots are something you can always start collecting now. They mean even more if they're passed down through the family.

WE HEART DRYER SHEETS, AND YOU SHOULD, TOO

Why, you ask? Here are some things this little multi-tasker can do.

- Hang a sheet outside to repel mosquitoes
- Stash one in our gym locker, sneaks, closet, desk drawer, car, and so on to soak up smells
- Rub one over pet hairs to pick them up
- Wipe your dress with a sheet to remove static cling
- Dust your TV and computer screens
- Clean shower doors
- Remove baked food from a pan (just add hot water and one dryer sheet!)

Look to walls for extra storage space. Line your living room walls with simple bracket shelves. Hang them two feet from the ceiling so they're high enough to display books and mementos but low enough to clean.

For a high fashion rug without the cost, buy a solid cotton dhurrie at any big box store. Fabric paint and a foam brush is all you need for DIY chevron stripes or a zebra print.

Learn how to reupholster your own pieces by looking up a YouTube video or by emailing a local shop that does it. Ask them to teach you the lost art in exchange for a week of bitch work.

Go bold with paint—but don't over do it. If you've always wanted a magenta bedroom, keep the rest of your walls a neutral shade.

Use your clothes or jewelry as décor. Hang necklaces from a doorknob or put your favorite sequin mini in a frame for a bit of glitz throughout the home.

ORGANIZING IDEAS

Push thumbtacks into a bulletin board and hang your necklaces from each one.

Don't let your drunchies (drunk munchies) go stale— binder clips double as great chip bag clips.

Group like items together in your medicine cabinet and store anything you wouldn't want a snooping guest to see underneath the sink, in a bag, in a bigger bag.

Forget the loose coin jar; if you store change in a plastic bag, it'll take up less space and it's easier to throw in your bag when it comes time to cashing in at the bank or at a Coinstar machine.

Traveling for a night? Pack your birth control pill, daily Lexapro dose, and what have you in a contact lens case so you can leave all the bottles and packs at home.

Designate a basket as your clutter keeper. Once a week, take it on a walk around your place, picking up any misplaced objects or un-hung clothes. As you walk into the next room, put back anything from your basket that belongs there.

Keep extension cords and other tangle-riffic wires bound neatly together behind the TV by slipping them through a cardboard toilet paper roll. Wanna get sexy with it? Label each roll with what the cord belongs to (cable box, Blu-ray, PlayStation, etc.).

If your dresser can't hold your clothes, try rolling pants and t-shirts and stacking them.

When you're editing your closets, go with the "love it," "kinda like it," "totally hate it" system to narrow down the keepers, the goners, and the maybes.

Don't bother organizing your closet by color. It won't last. Instead, every time you wear something, move it to the back so you can keep your closet revolving.

Use the inside of kitchen cupboards to post recipes, bills or any other reminders. They'll be easy to see and will look a lot prettier than Post-Its all over the place.

When it comes to kitchen cabinets, keep everything you use on a daily basis in one cabinet. Put plates, glasses, coffee mugs on one shelf so they're easy to grab. You can designate the rest to appropriately organized spots.

Always have a stack of paper cocktail napkins on hand. Also striped straws, though not as essential.

Though you should be shopping with a canvas tote, save your plastic grocery bags if you don't. They're a total pain in the ass for the environment if you trash them, and you can most certainly find a reason to reuse them in the future. Stash in an empty tissue box under the sink.

Hang some of your pretty pans and colanders on the kitchen wall. It's a cheap way to decorate and maybe you'll cook more.

Sell any appliances you don't use on Craigslist. Take that $25 you'll get from the never-been-touched slow cooker and treat yourself and girlfriends to sushi chez vous.

Every smart gal should have a file system. A simple accordion holder should be sectioned off for credit card bills, car payments, student loans, rent checks, and any other bills.

Hang a chalkboard or pretty cork board by your door. Leave yourself to-do lists or positive reinforcements to start the day off organized and perky.

Use a bookshelf as a shoe shelf. Fill with your heels, boots, and flats and fasten a fabric cover on the front. Or have two and have them double as a nightstand

Force yourself to purge your closet and have a clothing swap. Have friends bring over a garbage bag of clothes, swap, and donate whatever is left over to charity. Plus you'll save money on clothes for next season.

No medicine cabinet? No problem. Hang a mirror and a small shelf under it for your daily face wash, toothbrush and toothpaste, and moisturizer. The rest can go in a drawer or under the sink.

Keep a few small dishes—think porcelain used for soy sauce—around the apartment. Use them as drop off spots for loose change or jewelry.

Don't get caught in the paper chase. If you have trouble tossing notes, cards, or receipts, put them all in a file box but promise to go through them every month to cut down on the clutter.

Designate "daily wears" to your closet and dresser; and "out of season" items under your bed.

Does your bookshelf look like a college bookstore with "used" stickers along the binding? We thought so. Chances are you'll never read those again, so sell them to poor undergrads on campusbooks.com and make yourself a buck.

If you find yourself thinking about renting a storage space for your extra stuff, you've got too much crap. Time to visit Goodwill or have a stoop sale.

Do you have a junk drawer? Or bin? We know it's impossible to rid yourself of one, but make a biannual pillage to lessen the size. If you've gotten it down to a junk shoebox, you're in good shape.

Real Chick Tip

Don't ignore the signs of rodents. My first mouse spotting was just before a long weekend away. By the time I got back I was convinced they had taken over my apartment. I put traps everywhere and was barely sleeping. I came home from work one night, cracked open a beer, and started making my meal of choice—a cheese quesadilla—on the stove. I was chatting with my boyfriend when I looked back at my almost done meal and saw red stuff toward the back of the stove. It looked like red paint that had definitely not been there a minute earlier. Upon closer inspection, I saw a tail sticking out. The mouse was cut, bleeding, and struggling for its life while trapped in the area above the burners! We jumped on chairs, left the quesadilla, and called my brother. He ripped apart the stove and couldn't find the damn mouse. I moved two months later.

–Laura C., 28, NYC, financial recruiter

SECRETS FROM A STYLIST

Laura Fenton, prop stylist whose work has appeared in *Good Housekeeping* and *Country Living* magazines, tells us how to fake it till we make it:

1. **Ask Mom's advice—seriously!** Mom (or Dad) has a lot of experience setting up a house and may have some good ideas for you. Plus, your mom can veto trendy-today pieces that are likely to go out of style.

2. **Start an inspiration file.** If you're unsure of your tastes and style, start collecting photos of rooms you like. As your file of inspiration images grows, you'll be able to see your personal style emerge.

3. **Double Duty.** Every piece of furniture you purchase for your home should be both attractive and functional.

4. **Arrange bookshelves in a way that is pleasing to the eye,** interspersing favorite objects with your books. Use magazine holders to store your favorite gossip rags.

5. **Invest in the best.** When shopping for furniture, look for high-quality pieces with simple, classic designs. You may only have room for a loveseat now, but that doesn't mean you should buy the cheapest one you can.

6. **Black and white is always right.** If you're stumped for a color scheme, don't resort to boring beige. Instead, stick to a basic palette of black and white for a polished look that will match any colors you have now or ones you introduce in the future.

7. **Paint it!** A coat of glossy, white (or black) paint can transform almost any piece of furniture. Always sand and prime before you paint.

8. **Say yes to slipcovers.** If you inherited an ugly couch and can't afford a new one, invest in a ready-make slipcover. Visit surefit.com.

9. **Don't settle for ugly lighting.** Simple, affordable fixes can improve the look of your light fixtures: A coat of white or black spray paint can transform a hideous brass fixture.

10. **Mix old and new.** Incorporate a few vintage pieces into your décor to give your home some interest and texture.

11. **Ugly tiles in the rental bathroom?** A white shower curtain, white towels, and white walls can neutralize the offender.

12. **Reprint your photographs in black and white.** Spray-paint a bunch of mismatched frames in one hue for a pulled-together arrangement.

13. **Faux-get about it.** If you can't afford real hardwood furniture, it's better to opt for a finish that doesn't pretend to be something it isn't, like plain white melamine. Wood-like and stone-like finishes always look cheap.

SHAKE YOUR BOOTY DURING CLEANING DUTY

Play these tunes so you can cut a rug . . . while you vacuum it.

1. *My Old Ways*—Dr. Dog

2. *So What*—Pink

3. *I Kissed A Girl*—Katy Perry

4. *Dog Days Are Over*—Florence and the Machine

5. *You're So Vain*—Carol King

6. *Little Red Corvette*—Prince

7. *Like a Prayer*—Madonna

8. *Private Eyes*—Hall & Oates

9. *Bad Romance*—Lady Gaga

10. *Call Me Maybe*—Carly Rae Jepsen

LOVE & SEX

"I CAN LIVE WITHOUT MONEY, BUT I CANNOT
LIVE WITHOUT LOVE."

—*Judy Garland*

Perhaps there is no topic more important to the twentysome-thing girl than love and sex. These two often go hand in hand, like peanut butter and jelly, hot cocoa and marshmallows, Marky Mark and the Funky Bunch. Either way, the modern girl isn't coy about sex. We're happy to talk to our friends about our latest romps—both good and bad—and when it comes to love, we aren't afraid to discuss that either. So have no fear, we've been through the wringer (and back again) and we're ready to share our best advice that only our girlfriends get to hear. (But again, we're all about the quickies—punny, right?—so if you're looking for lengthy sex instructions, pounce elsewhere.)

FALLING IN LOVE

Be mindful of how your new flame fits into your life. Gets along with your friends? Check. Likes dogs? Check. Hates cupcakes? DEAL BREAKER! Just kidding. But pay attention to what matters to you.

Don't change your day-to-day. Just because you're in a relationship doesn't mean skipping out on hot yoga or your craft club.

Keep the chats about your SO to a minimum. When you're around friends and you start to notice eye rolling, it's probably because you've been rambling.

Have you been through the rigmarole before? Keep a running list—mental or physical—of all your deal breakers. Don't ignore it if one comes up. The more aware you are of what type of love you need, the more the universe will bring.

There shouldn't be a lot of questions surrounding it. If you find yourself wondering if it's too good to be true, it'll turn out that way! Embrace it, girl.

Remember your friends. A very common error when being in the honeymoon stage is to get wrapped up in it. Don't cancel on your women to stay in with your lover.

Try and resist finding out about your new love's past relationships. If you can't control your curiosity, say something along the lines of, "I'm only asking because I'm interested in the people who have been in your life!"

Did you let out a toot in bed? Oh, the embarrassment! Rather than ignore it, say "Oh dear. Now you know I'm human."

You don't need to wait for your new flame to drop the l-bomb. Try dropping it casually first with a "Love ya" before you hang up the phone.

Have a great makeout sesh followed by a lackluster first time? Not to worry. It doesn't have to be all fireworks and foreplay the first time, give it a few more. If the chemistry still isn't vibing after several tries, yikes.

SIGNS IT MIGHT NOT BE L-O-V-E

If you find yourself asking your friends a lot of questions about the relationship, you're confused about it. Breathe. Take a step back. And give yourself a week to analyze it without asking for a second opinion.

Acting differently or taking up new hobbies in order to please your partner isn't necessary. If they're only going to love you if you listen to Bon Jovi, then they can take their copy of *Slippery When Wet* and shove it.

If there are any signs of abuse—physical, emotional, or mental—there are no excuses. That ain't love, honey.

Stay in the same room when you argue. It'll force you both to talk it out and it will cut down on shouting.

Pay attention to how he or she relates to your friends. Does your SO make a true effort to know them? Do they ask your friends questions? Do your friends like this person? "I guess" just isn't good enough when it comes to how they treat the people you love.

If you find that most of your phone calls or text messages are being answered after 10pm, you are probably not a priority. Don't fall for the "but I've been so busy at work" line. If he or she is interested, they'll make time.

Don't allow a person to create rifts in your life. If a friend has felt like you aren't yourself around that person, don't get mad at them. Instead, pay attention.

MAINTAINING

It's been said over and over again that men are attracted to certain scents: cinnamon, vanilla, and lavender. Maybe it's time for a new candle or perfume?

There is a fine line between nagging and asking for help. If your guy isn't interested in doing the dishes, insist he'll have to pick up the slack with laundry or another chore.

Don't let the romance die. It isn't just up to our partners to surprise us with roses or make the first move in bed. It's the twenty-first century, ladies! Make a favorite meal or offer up a foot rub and chances are, your partner will reciprocate.

It's easy to take advantage of the person you're with as time goes on, so make sure you take the time to have meaningful conversations. Keep the TV off during dinner and instead hash out how your day went.

On a random Tuesday night after your late night shower, don't dry off. Put on a white t-shirt and head to bed. You'll find your partner speechless.

Every couple gets in a rough patch or two—or eighteen. But don't panic right away. It's important to learn how to argue with your significant other so you can get through the tough stuff.

To get in the mood after a dismal day at the office, hit the spa for a quick massage. Touch is the trigger that releases oxytocin—the feel-good, anti-stress hormone—which in turn, will leave you wanting more.

Keep mints in your nightstand. Pop one in your mouth right before bed—and again right when you wake up. No morning breath for you.

Write each other love letters and hide them in a drawer. When you get in a big fight, read them in separate rooms and then come back together. Sometimes you just need a reminder.

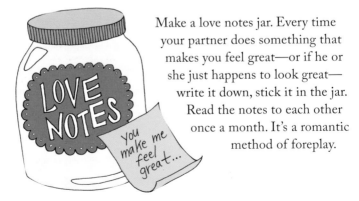

Make a love notes jar. Every time your partner does something that makes you feel great—or if he or she just happens to look great—write it down, stick it in the jar. Read the notes to each other once a month. It's a romantic method of foreplay.

The following texts always work:
I want to be on top of you.
The thought of you makes me hot.
Hurry home after work. I plan on pleasing you.
Wanna bang?

Be spontaneous. There's nothing worse than stopping a hot and heavy moment because you've realized you haven't shaved your legs. Just go for it.

Don't argue in public. Ever see that go down in Target? Totally embarrassing. Wait until you get home.

Studies show the smell of pumpkin pie turns women on. A good reason to order dessert, for once!

Kiss like you mean it. Close your eyes and hold that moment for five seconds before heading to work in the morning. Make that kiss count.

Leave dirty notes in unexpected places, like on a car windshield.

Keeping the passion alive isn't about squeezing your body into sexy lingerie. It's about passion. Does your girlfriend's smile turn you on? Tell her. Do your man's skills in the kitchen get you going? Let him know. Nothing's sexier than that.

No sneaking into your lover's inbox, Facebook account, or bank accounts.

Use The Sex Positions Finder at ivillage.com if your routine is in need of a shake-up.

Shouts and pouts are out. Say that to yourself. Nobody wants to date an eight-year-old.

Meet at the movies, a bar, anywhere that isn't your home. It'll feel like a first date when you have the anticipation of walking into a public place and spotting your honey.

A LESSON IN LOVE

Meg Fee, the blogger behind *Wild & Wily Ways of a Brunette Bombshell,* writes notes to her future husband on her blog. Here she shares the biggest lesson she's learned (so far) in her twenties.

"I've been thinking about love stories of late and how we all have one—probably more than one. And how each is different. Truly, each love story is singular. The stranger who smiles across the crowded D train, a love story born and done in the same moment. I'm no good at some of the more traditional love stories. The great love of my life has not been easy or linear. It has stretched years and uncomfortable silences and to those outside it seems, dare I say it, ridiculous. **But what I've learned it is this: it is for no person to judge another's relationship.** It is for no person to condemn another's love story. We all try to, to judge, and to compare, and to measure our own tale against another's—but nothing is more pointless or futile, or painful really. So what I know now is I must listen to my gut, to my own surprisingly resilient heart."

Use lots of "I" statements instead of "you" statements. If you're trying to express something that is making you unhappy, explain how you're feeling rather than point out what you think the other person is doing wrong.

If you're out for dinner or away on vacay celebrating something—an anniversary, a birthday, a job promotion—tell your waiter or the front desk. You may score a free bottle of wine or some other romantic goody.

Want to get better at doing the deed? Do yoga—it increases flexibility and endurance, and teaches you to enjoy—and live in—the moment.

BACK IN THE GAME

If you've taken some time off from finding Mr. or Mrs. Right, Tina Tessina, PhD, "Dr. Romance" and author of *Money, Sex, and Kids: Three Things That Can Ruin Your Marriage*, tells us how to find it the right way.

- Do "shop around." Don't stay focused on one person until you've given yourself a choice.

- Do focus on friendship. This early, you can't know where it might go, so concentrate on developing the friendship. You can have as many friends as you want.

- Do get feedback. Offer your comments on the event or the restaurant, and ask your date what he or she thought of it, for future reference.

- Do let your date know if you enjoyed his/her company. A compliment is always welcome. If you'd like to do it again, say so. If you promise to call, mean it.

- Do tell the truth, but also don't share too much too soon. You don't need to tell your date about other dates if you two have no agreement about exclusivity.

LET'S TALK ABOUT SEX, BABY

Foreplay is great. It's really important to any intimate act. But is it always necessary? Nope. Sometimes a quickie in the shower is all you need to start the day off right.

Try getting it on without saying a word. There's always a time and place for dirty talk but hushing up and letting the other senses feel heightened is just as good.

Don't do something you don't want to do. Period. That doesn't mean you have to be totally closed off to a topic either. If your partner wants to try a potentially compromising position (literally) then ease into it and try some simpler positions first.

Don't pay attention to your number. So you're creeping into the double digits, big deal! Or you've only slept with one person? Who cares? Sex is all about satisfaction, not a particular checklist you need to mark off.

It's quality over quantity, ladies. You can't really compare yourself to any other couple ("Holy crap— they do it *EVERY NIGHT.*") but you do have to ask yourself if you're feeling fulfilled. If you are, then there's nothing to worry about.

Say you can't get to Plan B after a sex emergency. There are some birth control pills you can double up on as an alternative—ask your doctor if yours is one of those kinds.

You gotta give head to get head. It's true. Oral sex is great, but it's also a two-way street. And if you're giving and not getting, speak up. You're missing out.

How to have an ideal one-night stand: No emotion. Total safety. Don't expect breakfast in the a.m. In fact, go home when you're done. And most importantly, no regrets—we've all had at least one.

Safety isn't overrated. Whether you're sleeping with many partners or just a longtime love, take precaution. If you aren't ready to have a baby or catch something scarier than a cold, wrap it up!

Did you have a wild weekend and left with the smell of sex? Sprinkle some baking powder on that bed, couch, or back of the car.

Compliment your partner the first time you see them naked. It's something they'll always remember and it will offer a major ego boost and will most definitely result in better sex.

You like something in the bedroom? Say it. If you're shy, text it to your lover. Just make sure you're open about what you want between the sheets.

If you're thinking about "baring" it, shave with the blade against the hair growth—not with it.

Do you taste better downtown if you eat certain foods? Well, you are what you eat. We'd suggest some kiwi and pineapple (and some sources say lots of green veggies) and avoid stinky things like cigarettes and burritos.

Your body isn't what you want it to be? Don't take that insecurity into the bedroom, girl! Trust us, no one will care if you have a pooch when you're on top. Plus, high-waisted briefs are in again!

Comfort is key when it comes to a sexual relationship. You'll be more ready to try new things if you're at ease with your partner.

Real Chick Tip

Find someone with the same experience level as you—or somewhere close to it. I had a summer fling with an old co-worker and came to discover that he was a virgin. A thirty-two-year-old virgin. I thought long and hard before whether or not I should take on the challenge. Should I get a hotel room and sprinkle rose petals on the bed? Should we set a date? Should we just let it happen naturally? Should we start with the missionary position? Do we high-five after? In the end, I feel like I ruined his first time. I was tipsy, I pulled a muscle, and I thought he finished before he actually did. I am a horrible deflowerer! I did make it up to him though and I've learned to stick with men that have just as much experience as me in the bedroom.

—Amanda, 28, CT, teacher

Whipped cream, handcuffs,
cool. But know what excites
another person more than
anything? Nudity.

MY BEST SEX ADVICE

Who better to dole out some bedroom dynamics other than the anonymous sex blogger behind *Between My Sheets*? She's letting us in on her very best bedroom behavior—and misbehavior.

- Sometimes you have to take the initiative, especially if you're in a relationship where sex isn't deemed very important. No one likes to be rejected, so if you've constantly told your man no, he's going to eventually stop trying. When you are feeling frisky, don't be shy about it. Make the first move. Most will be totally receptive—they just need a signal.

- Watch porn together. Yes, porn! I know for a lot of couples that sounds really raunchy and kind of embarrassing, but it can actually be really hot. You don't even have to buy it. There's plenty of porn available online for free. You can mimic some of their moves, but more importantly, it gives you both an opening to talk about your fantasies.

- Don't be afraid to pick up a few toys for the bedroom. If you're too embarrassed to go to a local adult store, just shop online—everything is shipped discreetly, so you don't have to worry about your neighbors seeing UPS drop off your new vibrator. Shop together for something that makes you both hot.

- Nothing sucks the sex out of a relationship faster than kids! So, start by setting some clear boundaries in your house. For example, your bedroom should only be a room the kids can enter if they have your permission/ knock. In addition, you should also try to have one night a week to yourselves. Squeeze in sex when your kids are none the wiser, like when you're showering in the morning.

THE MARRIAGE CHECKLIST

Marital therapist Leslie Beth Wish (lovevictory.com), columnist of Relationship Realities at QualityHealthy.com, weighs in on the things you should be thinking about (and asking yourself) before you take the marital plunge:

- Do I respect this person? And is the feeling mutual?

- Is our relationship a roller coaster ride of ups and downs? (Hint: It shouldn't be).

- Do we constantly bicker over little things—or do I find his/ her quirks as part of who he or she is?

- Do I have a laundry list of things I want to change about that person? Do I like my partner as is?

- Do we have major hurdles we've yet to figure out? Sex problems? If we want children? How we should manage our money for the future?

- Most importantly, do you like who you are in the relationship? Do you learn from the person you're with and value each of your different ways of thinking?

MONEY

"I NEED MONEY. YOU KNOW MONEY.
I NEED TO KNOW WHAT YOU
KNOW ABOUT MONEY."

—*Carrie Bradshaw*

Money, money everywhere, and we're barely earning any of it. Unless you created the next big thing in social media that the whole world is using (curse that Zuckerberg!), you're likely in the same boat as most twentysomethings at this point—getting by paycheck to paycheck, ecstatic when you find a crumpled $20 bill in your jeans pocket (isn't that the best?). From rent, daily expenses, dinners out, and the occasional splurge on a Tory Burch handbag, it's a monetary quicksand out there. Here's how to stay above ground, keeping your finances and future in tact, while still living the fabulous life. (We could tell you to avoid designer clothes, but we know that just isn't happening.)

HOW TO MANAGE YOUR MOOLAH AND MONTHLY EXPENSES

If you tend to overdraw your account often, hey it happens, ask your bank if they can link your account to your savings, so the money gets transferred out without you getting slapped with fees.

Check your debit and credit card accounts daily, so you know how much you owe or have spent lately, and if you need to replenish your checking account before using your debit again.

If you don't already have a go-to bank for all your accounts, consider the following: What's close by? What's the minimum deposit to start an account? Are there fees for online banking? Which ATMs can you use?

Take advantage of your company's 401k ASAP. If they match a certain percentage, that's free money. You decide how much to contribute, but even as little as 2% is worth it. Have no clue what it all means? Ask your HR specialist—or your parents—for help.

If you have a job, set up your paychecks to be deposited directly into your account. The worst thing you can ever do is receive a check, and forget to cash it in time. Plus, many banks won't charge a monthly billing fee if you use their direct deposit.

Sign up for free at Billguard.com. What it does: You provide the login info for your credit and debit card accounts (it's safe). It then scans your bills, looking for hidden fees, billing errors, anything fishy, and sends the report right away. Nice, right? No catch!

Keep most of your money in a savings account, with just enough in your checking to cover daily expenses. But when you write a big, fat check for something (rent, for example), make sure you have enough in your checking to cover it. Smart girls don't bounce checks. (That'll hurt your credit history.)

Utilize pre-tax dollars from your paycheck for current expenses, too. You've probably heard the terms "flexible spending account" and "transportation benefits." Signing up for flex spending basically means you can use pre-taxed money to pay for things like contact lenses. And say you ride public transportation to work, ask your employer about allotting part of your paycheck to the fees, pre-tax.

This should really go out without saying, but we'll say it anyway: Don't give your social security, bank account, or other important numbers to anyone. If you get an email asking for that info, it's most likely a fraud.

If you're the kind of person who forgets to pay bills on time, set up alerts. Either online or your mobile phone, where bill reminder apps abound.

Stay organized! Make folders for monthly expenses, bank statements, tax stuff (W2s, pay stubs, tax returns), and so on.

From financial aid letters to insurance policies to bank statements, if you don't know whether to toss it or save it, save it.

Invest in a paper shredder. If you're tossing something with critical info on it, like your credit card account number, shred it first. You can find shredders for as low as $15 on Amazon.com, or shredding scissors for even less.

See purchases on your bills that you didn't authorize? Lost a card? Call your company stat to report it. If identity theft is involved, get the police involved, too.

Here's the skinny on your credit score: It needs to be good, so you have no problem applying for mortgages, apartments, and what have you in the future. When you want to see it, only use annualcreditreport.com. Law requires that each of the three reporting companies (Equifax, TransUnion, and Experian) provides you with a free copy once a year, and that site is where you can obtain them.

... And no, you don't have to get all three copies at the same time. One pretty much sums it up, but at least you have option of seeing the others. It's a good idea to request one at a time throughout the 12-month period, so you can keep tabs on how you're doing.

Forget the credit line numb on your credit card. Just beca you have a $4,000 credit lin doesn't mean you have tha much to blow. In fact, beg t keep your limit low.

And just so you know, your employer can see your credit report, but only if you allow it. For more details, the best resource is at ftc.gov (Federal Trade Commission).

GET A HANDLE ON YOUR FINANCES WITH MINT.COM

There's a reason people are obsessed with Mint.com, an Intuit company. It's a girl's best friend when it comes to budgeting and so much more. So we had Barb Chang, personal finance expert from Mint.com, share her favorite tips and site features for ladies like us.

1. **Preparation:** Plan ahead for big costs like tuition, books, and housing. *(Resource: Use Mint.com's Goals feature for a step-by-step guide helping you manage payments and expectations for set goals.)*

2. **Set a budget:** List out all expected expenses where you can't control the cost (rent) and figure out how much you have left over for things where you can control the costs (shopping and eating out at restaurants). *(Resource: Use Mint.com to track spending and be alerted when you are close to going over budget.)*

3. **Be careful with credit cards:** Credit cards can actually be a good thing, since they help you build a solid credit history to show the world that you can take on debt and can pay it back promptly. *(Resource: Mint.com's Ways to Save can help you track your credit card spending and recommend credit cards with rewards and cash back incentives)*

4. **Student Loans:** With student loan default rates soaring and 11.2% of student loans currently more than ninety days past due, it is important to stay on top of your payments during and after college. *(Resource: Use Mint's Student Loans goal to breakdown payments and create an action plan.)*

WHAT IN THE WORLD IS A 401(K), ANYWAY?

In its most basic terms, it's a tax-deferred retirement savings plan sponsored by your employer. You can elect to put a certain amount from your paychecks into this account, and at some point, hopefully, your employer will match your contributions. In other words, you're saving for the future, babe! Our hottest 401(k) tip: If you're in desperate need for fast cash, withdrawing early should be your last resort, if one at all. It's expensive! Penalties, taxes . . . Do everything you can to wait 'til your sexy sixties to reap the rewards. (Oh, and if you change jobs, roll it over to your new account . . . keeps everything easy to access).

Student loans. Sigh. Quickest tips we have for you on this subject: Keep track of your balance. Know your grace period (how long you have post-grad to make your first payment), and if you're ever in serious hot water, know that there are options. Ask your financial advisor (or parents . . .) about "deferments" and "forbearance."

"EVRYONE WANTS TO RIDE WITH YOU IN THE LIMO, BUT WHAT YOU WANT IS SOMEONE WHO WILL TAKE THE BUS WITH YOU WHEN THE LIMO BREAKS DOWN."
— OPRAH WINFREY

Only open a store credit card if you honestly shop there all the time. The incentives to join are tempting, but eventually canceling these cards can actually hurt your credit score. If you do have a card that's paid off but you no longer use, cut it up but don't cancel it, to keep your credit score up.

Real Chick Tip

Don't ignore (or be overwhelmed by!) your student loans. When my first bill arrived, I looked at the total balance due and was completely overwhelmed—I'm paying how much a month for how many years?! Very quickly I realized it was necessary (for both my bank account and my sanity) to treat these loans just like my other monthly, necessary expenses—like gas and rent. With just a little extra budgeting effort, I found the money. And with a few deep breaths, I learned to push the "40 years to go!" thoughts out of my head.

–Ashley, 29, NY, social media specialist

SAVE, SAVE, SAVE

Shopping online? Start at a site that offers rebates, like ebates.com. How it works: Log in to your free account, look for the site you want to buy from (example: victoriassecret.com), then click. You'll be taken to that site, but ebates.com will track your purchase. If you buy, you'll end up getting a certain percentage back in the form of a check from ebates.com.

Need to lay off the credit card for a few weeks? Freeze it. No, for real. Fill a bowl with water, dunk it in and put it in the freezer. Next time you're feeling to the urge to splurge, you'll have to consider if the purchase is worth the labor of literally cracking it free.

Do *not* go to the grocery store on an empty stomach. You'll end up detouring from your list and spending more dough on crap you wouldn't have bought otherwise. Instead, shop when you're in a hurry so you don't linger at the bakery, contemplating straying from your list.

Don't store your credit card numbers online. Do that, and it's a little too easy to click buy and be done with a purchase in a snap. If you don't have your number stored and you don't have it memorized, it gives you time to decide if you really need the item or not.

If you've got some crazy fear of going to the bathroom at work and try to hold it until your home, face it down ASAP. Hey, free resources! Those toilet paper rolls add up.

Before you click "buy" online, anywhere you are, always search the site you're buying from, plus "promo code," "coupon code," or some variation on that. Scour the depths of the Internet until you find one. Bookmark the site retailmenot.com as a go-to.

Really can't find one a code? Spend a few seconds guessing. Often times, retailers' codes are a combo of the current season and a percent off. Example: spring15. Try a few combos and you may get lucky.

Be as green as you can be at home. Turn off lights, unplug devices when not in use, and replace your bulbs with LEDs— they last longer.

Watch the register whenever you check out somewhere—the grocery store, J Crew. Mistakes happen, and it's often up to you to catch them.

As you roam the aisles in the supermarket, look high and low. Lots of times the pricier stuff is placed directly at eye level on purpose. And pay close attention to endcaps—you may think they're advertising a good deal, but it's not always so.

Fill an empty water bottle with pebbles and water, then place it in your toilet's water tank. This trick displaces water, ultimately saving up to a gallon with each use.

Call your cable company and say the magic words: "I'm considering canceling my service and switching to a *dish* network to save money." You'll be transferred to a special "cancellation" department, where a trained employee will lower your rate like it's his, uh, job.

Better yet, cancel cable. You can watch nearly any movie or show for free these days. Check hulu.com, the channel's main site, or a Google search for a legal source that's streaming the flick.

Libraries aren't just for books. Use your card to rent DVDs for free.

Also, make Redbox kiosks (those $1 movie dispensers often found in grocery stores) your friend. At insideredbox.com, you'll find codes for free movies.

When your loose change jar is overflowing, roll those coins the old-fashioned way with papers from the bank. Yes, Coinstar machines are fun, but when you get cash for your change, they take 9.8 cents per dollar counted. That adds up, yo!

Really, really want something . . . but don't necessarily need it? Follow the three-night rule: Sleep on it for three nights, then decide if you can't live without it.

Listen to music for free at grooveshark.com or spotify.com.

Lower your AC or heater just a bit, and rely more on light clothing or heavy blankets, respectively. A few degrees can mean big savings on your bills.

Freeshipping.org. Bookmark it.

Whenever you park, position your car so that when you're ready to leave, you can go forward and keep driving (instead of backing out of the spot, which actually uses more gas than the alternative).

Get social! Retailers tweet discounts, post Facebook-exclusive deals, and create Foursquare check-in specials. Follow all your favorite brands to be in the know.

Sign up to free customer rewards programs. From CVS and Panera to local restaurants and movie theatres, so many places offer the program for zilch and surprise you with coupons and freebies.

Stop buying bottled H20! The average American blows over $100 per year on water bottles, when (hello!) water is free. And pssst . . . some bottled water companies are literally just bottling tap water and making it look pretty. Invest in a thermos and never leave its sight.

Real Chick Tip

Bring lunch. One of the easiest ways to save money is to pack your lunch for work rather than buy a salad or sandwich for $10. Even bringing your lunch three days a week will help you save up to $30 (that's $1,560 a year!). Mix up your routine, making sure that the meal can be either easily assembled at work or won't get overly soggy throughout the day. Some of my favorites: quinoa with roasted butternut squash, walnuts, and dried cranberries; spinach with chickpeas, parmesan, and avocado; and fusilli with lemon zest, roasted asparagus, and peas.

–Olivia, 26, NY, journalist

DOWNLOAD IT!

These smartphone apps are must-haves for any budget-conscious babe.

GasBuddy—Low on fuel? Find the cheapest gas near you.

RedLaser Barcode Scanner and QR Code Reader—Scan the barcode of what you're about to buy, and this app will show you where to get it for less money.

AroundMe—Use this to locate specific ATMs wherever you are. Never again pay an ATM fee!

Yipit Deals: Daily Deals, Sales, and Coupons—You know Groupon, LivingSocial, and all those other daily deal sites? Yeah, there are a lot. Yipit brings them all in one place for you.

Retailmenot—Find a huge variety of online and in-store coupons for your favorite stores.

RepairPal: Auto Repair Expert—Before you pay what a mechanic asks of you, get a fair estimate here. Let's be real; unless you grew up around cars, it's very possible you'll be taken for a ride whenever you need a repair.

IF IT'S FREE, IT'S FOR ME

These days, free samples and gratis stuff are pretty much everywhere you look. Here's your freebie-snatching starter kit:

- Heyitsfree.net, shop4freebies.com, and freesamplemomma.com collect free sample offers.

- Wherever you go on your birthday—from Starbucks to Sephora—tell 'em it's your birthday to see if you get a freebie.

- Take advantage of local trade schools; beauty schools, for example, might offer free haircuts in return for your being a guinea pig for students.
- Swap books for other books at paperbackswap.com.
- Freecycle.org is another good resource to find free stuff in your area that people are giving way.

LIVE LIKE A ROCK STAR, PAY LIKE A GROUPIE

You can still eat at fabulous restaurants every now and again, but always scour the Web first for coupons. Also check restaurant.com, where you can nab gift certificates ($25 for just $10, for example) to over 18,000 spots across the US.

Put cash in an envelope at the start of each week—as much as you can afford on discretionary spending—and when you run out, you run out. Replenish next week.

Wanna feel like a big-shot philanthropist without any cash? A few options: Help hunger for free by answering vocab questions at freerice.com; donate blood at your local hospital; volunteer your time (find opportunities at volunteeermatch.org); chop your hair for Locks of Love; and help provide free mammograms to women by simply clicking your mouse at thebreastcancersite.com. (Also see theautismsite.com, thechildhealthsite.com, and all their other partner sites that require only clicks).

If you've got a side biz, get yourself some rockin' biz card At vistaprint.com, the first 20 you print are totally free, plu the cost of shipping.

An accounting survey showed that young professionals, eighteen to thirty-four, spend about $24.74 on coffee during the week. You do the math. Get your coffee fix as much as you'd like, but make it at home to save bucks.

Rock a superstar body by running outside, lifting dumbbells at home, and using fitness DVDs. If you really want a gym membership, at least compare prices before signing up for one. If you don't go to the gym more than three times the first month of your membership, cancel it.

If you see a snag in the fabric or a missing button or anything wrong with the piece you're looking to buy, for the love of God, point it out to a sales associate for a deeper discount.

Never underestimate the quality of clothes at Marshall's and TJ Maxx. Their inventory comes from great brand names who need to move excess merch. Start hunting!

If you see something online that you love from a store you don't normally shop at, sign up for their emails. You'll often receive a "Thanks for subscribing. Save 15% Off Your Order" email right away that you can use to snag that dress!

Listen, outlets are great for savings. But hear this: Not everything is a good deal. In fact, a lot of retailers create pieces exclusively for the outlets, so they're not even marked down from an "original" price. Really decide if what you're eyeing is worth the price.

When you'd kill to have that cable-knit sweater, that charming loveseat, that trendy tote, or that killer rug: negotiate. Ask to speak to a manager or someone who can authorize discounts. Be polite. Ask if paying cash instead of credit will get you a deal. Say something like, "If I buy two, can I get one half off?" Ask about upcoming sales, and basically, just ask how you can save money right now. Employees get it; they want to save money, too.

 Planning a fancy, schmancy date with your significant other? Consider going out just for dessert, not a full meal.

And when you're out dining, order water . . . the cost of soda is typically jacked up at restaurants, and you're there for the food—not the beverages. Unless you're out for the wine, in which case, ask for the house to save some change.

You can have a packed social calendar without shilling out cash at every event. Keep your ears open for free events—gallery openings, concerts, art fairs—and use myopenbar.com to find drink specials in various cities.

HEY, JETSETTERS . . .

We put all our juicy tips on how to save on travel in the travel chapter. Page 251.

HOLY CREDIT CARD DEBT!

Say you got yourself into a bit of a pickle. You got carried away with the plastic at your disposal, and now you owe more than you have. Let us introduce you to the daughter of renowned finance guru Dave Ramsey: Rachel Cruze, another pro on all things money and a speaker for the Dave Ramsey Group (daveramsey.com). Follow her attack strategy below:

1. Get on a plan. It's a powerful feeling when you tell your money what to do. Right now, cut up your credit cards, stop going into debt, and create a budget.

2. Start an emergency fund. Each paycheck going forward, put a little bit towards it every month. This means you have to eliminate unnecessary expenses. It takes about three months for the average person to build up a strong emergency fund. When you're at $1,000, you're ready for step 3.

3. Begin paying off debts, starting with the smallest— regardless of interest rates. Personal finance is 80 percent behavior, 20 percent head knowledge. When you knock out that first small debt, you'll feel encouraged to continue.

4. Learn to say no. The whole idea of getting out of debt is a freeing concept, but it takes willpower to turn down, say, a steal of a jacket. Need more motivation? Write your debts out and tape it to the fridge. Once you pay off the first one, put a big red line through it.

5. Get intense. Making the minimum payments is essential, but the quicker you rid yourself of debt, the sooner you're in the clear. Get a part-time job if you need to. Just get intense and get past it, one debt at a time.

MAKE EXTRA CASH PRONTO

Bi-weekly paychecks just ain't cuttin' it? Bring in some more bucks with these ideas:

- Sell your stuff on eBay or Craigslist, or your handiwork on Etsy.

- Return things you recently bought. Even if you don't have a receipt, just try it. Often times, stores will let you show proof of payment to get the return.

- Throw a yard sale, and promote it on all your social spaces.

- Find paying focus groups at, well, findfocusgroups.com.

- Submit photos to stock photo sites, like shutterstock.com or istockphoto.com. If they sell, you earn money.

- Check out mturk.com, Amazon Mechanical Turk. Companies post random tasks they need done—some only take a few hours—and will pay you in return for your help.

TRAVEL

"WE TRAVEL, SOME OF US FOREVER,
TO SEEK OTHER STATES,
OTHER LIVES, OTHER SOULS."

—*Anaïs Nin*

Bon voyage, darlings! A twentysomething's life should be full of exciting travels. But with spring break in the rear view mirror, we're adults now. We need to keep our budgets in mind, our bodies safe, and our brains in frazzle-free mode if we're going to enjoy ourselves at all. Whether you're checking the box next to business or pleasure, there are lots of ways to make the most of your getaway and travel smart. And we're off!

THE PLANNING PART

Plan your flight to arrive during the day if you're riding solo.

Follow #TravelTuesday on Twitter to get updates on deals galore.

Write your first name, email address, and phone number on an index card, with this message: "If you find this camera, call me!" Then take a pic of the card. Should you lose your camera, pray that whoever finds it heeds your plea.

Here's the deal on all those booking travel sites out there: Orbitz, Expedia, and others like them are one set, while Kayak, Mobissimo, and Sidestep are another. The latter are comparison sites, which can save you time and money by searching all those deal sites out there simultaneously.

According to farecompare.com, the best time to buy airline tickets is on Tuesdays—at 3pm Eastern to be exact.

If you don't already know a travel agent, describe your dream trip at pricesfortravel.com and let agents bid for your service with proposed itineraries and prices.

Glitches happen. If you're trying to book a ridiculously low-priced flight online and it's not letting you, snap a photo of the price and hit print. That way, when the site's back up and so is the price, you have evidence to use when you call and bitch them out.

Flying for a funeral? We're sorry. Call the airline directly and ask if they offer a "bereavement rate," for which you may have to provide some proof. But remember: these fares may still be higher than others you can find, so still do your research.

Add an embellishment to your luggage so you can easily spot it at baggage claim. A cute ribbon, colorful masking tape…

Make two photocopies each of your passport, license, debit card, credit card, and travel itinerary (with reservation numbers and flight info). Keep one set with you, and give the other to a parent or pal who's not traveling with you.

If your trip requires a fairly complicated itinerary or it's a huge deal—like a honeymoon or two-month safari—it's probably worth it to work with a travel agent. (And get this: not all charge clients for their services!)

Call your phone service and tell them where you're headed. Turn off the data feature to avoid sky-high bills, and ask about reduced-price texting.

If you'll be gone for several weeks or longer, ask your phone, Internet, and utility providers about "scasonal rates" or "vacation service suspensions."

Either stop your mail or have a neighbor pick it up. If you leave your papers accumulating out front, thieves will take note.

You know that [insert five-pound travel guide book] you love? Yeah, you don't need the whole dang thing. Photocopy the chapters or pages you want, and leave the rest at home. Or email excerpts to your iPhone, iPad, and other handy travel gadget.

Traveling without any mans and as single as they come? Get a fake wedding-like ring to ward off strange men. Unless you're cruising for a cutie at the swim-up bar. In that case, slip it in your tote . . . but *be safe*!

GET PACKING

Perhaps one of the worst parts of traveling is the prep work of fitting all your essentials (and, okay, non-essentials) into your itty-bitty suitcase. Here to help is Los Angeles-based fashion expert, stylist, host, and blogger, Sydne Summer (sydnestyle.com), with her top five packing tips:

1. **Keep it in the (color) family.** Stick to one color palette per vacation to avoid overpacking. Black and white is the easiest—but blues or browns work, too. This way, you can bring less footwear and handbags and use jewelry, which is lighter and smaller, to switch up your outfits.

2. **Treat your baubles like bling.** A great way to organize jewelry is in a hanging cosmetic case. The plastic compartments make it easy to find your earrings or rings, which can get lost in traditional pouches.

3. **Roll it, don't fold it.** To avoid creasing, your best bet is to stick to travel-friendly fabrics like jersey and cotton. But if you absolutely must bring chiffon or silk, try rolling it! Lay the garment flat on your bed or a table. Layer a piece of tissue paper on top, and gently roll it up.

4. **Stuff your shoes.** To avoid sandals and boots losing their structure, stuff them with socks. This helps keep the shape, plus it will save you room when packing.

5. **Carry it on.** Always bring at least one extra outfit in your carry-on. The worst beginning to any vacation is your luggage getting lost and having nothing to wear! A jersey dress or even an extra top and statement necklace if your wearing jeans will hold you over until the airline can deliver your bags.

Real Chick Tip

Consider nontraditional travel as a chance to give back. There are lots of volunteer opportunities around the world that can promise adventure, empowerment, and a chance to bring your skills to a deserving organization. I was twenty years old the first time I volunteered globally. I helped rebuild a damaged castle in Scotland with other young people from across the world. The work was interesting and fun, but the connections I made with such an international group is something that I'll cherish forever. Since then I have been able to do similar projects, in Thailand and South Africa and elsewhere.

–Samantha N., 26, AZ, PR specialist

OH THE BEACHES YOU'LL GO . . .

We've got a resident expert on our hands. Melissa, co-author of this fine book, is semi-obsessed with all things tropical and loves to swap firsthand beach experiences with other picky travelers who love to kick back in a germaphobe-friendly, palm tree-packed place. She's never actually written down her favorite finds—until now. Can't decide where to go? Here are her picks:

IF YOU WANT…	GO HERE	WHAT IT'S LIKE	BEST PLACE TO STAY	ITEMS OF NOTE
A town you can walk around in	Playa Del Carmen, Mexico	Super cute area with a lot of smaller hotels and a main strip called 5th Avenue (Quinto Avenido) of restaurants and shops. Most of the hotels belong to beach clubs where you can get chairs and towels.	La Tortuga Hotel and Spa. A block away from the hubbub of 5th Avenue, and a few blocks from the beach—but it's a fun walk! Small pool, but you're there for the beach, right?	Lots of great info at iloveplaya.com. And get Thai food at Babe's Noodles. Omg, amazing.
An upgraded, but budget-friendly all-inclusive resort for you and your lovah	Punta Cana, Dominican Republic	You'll stay on the resort, and you won't mind at all. Beautiful pools, awesome beach, and the restaurants are really decent despite what you hear of all-inclusives.	Majestic Elegance. The drive there is sort of depressing, but when you arrive, you feel safe, tucked away, and totally in the romantic spirit.	Upgrade to the Elegance Club—the adults-only section with tons of extra amenities, so worth the extra price.
A fun all-inclusive for you and your ladies	Ocho Rios, Jamaica	Again, you won't wander off resort—but you won't need to. Lots of activities, bars, and shows to entertain yourselves.	The Riu Ocho Rios. The service was incredibly attentive, the rooms clean, and the resort sprawling.	Get to know the bartenders' names. They'll treat you extra special. This really goes for anywhere you travel …
Pure paradise and you've got money to burn	Turks & Caicos	Like I said, pure paradise.	Anywhere.	It's expensive.
A hidden gem away from the masses that's easy on your wallet	Cabarete, Dominican Republic	A row of restaurants and nightclubs dot one area of the beach, and it's safe to walk up and down. But stick to the beach side; the road side gets a little sketch.	For you and your mate: Cabarete Palm Beach Condos are spacious for the cheap price and in the middle of the action. For a huge group, split a villa down the street—the Bahia de Arena group of villas is clutch.	Kiteboarding is the thing to do here. If you're feeling athletic, give it a go!

EN ROUTE

Frisk yourself. Jewelry, belts, shades—put 'em all in your carry-on just in case.

Wear shoes you can easily slip on and off at security. Don't be that girl with laces to tie and untie.

Don't take pictures at the airport. Someone, somewhere, will ask you to delete the pic or even take your camera from you.

Have your boarding pass and ID easily accessible at all times, but in a place where it won't fall out, like the side pocket of your bag.

Not flexible with timing and your flight is delayed or cancelled? Immediately ask about "Rule 240 options." Long story short on this sometimes existent, sometimes-not contract clause (which you can read in-depth about online), the airline may be required to put you on a competitor's flight or comp you with hotel or meal vouchers.

Don't assume your tray table was wiped clean before you sat down. If you're going to use it, swipe it with an antibacterial wipe first.

Don't share a cab with anyone. Have you seen *Taken*? Liam Neeson will not be there to save you. Joking aside, you can never be too cautious when you travel.

When you to get to your gate, ask if the flight is overbooked. If it is, and you'd be okay with taking a later flight, get on the volunteer-to-bump list. Why? You may get some sweet perks—first-class on the next flight, free ticket, etc.

Real Chick Tip

When I travel, I never want to be one of the first people on the plane. For instance, with open seating, I always wait to check-in to ensure I am one of the later boarding groups. This way, I can avoid all of the parents with screaming kids and scope out the attractive guys with open middle seats. Don't be too late, or you can get stuck!

–Sharon, 23, MD,
communications & support specialist

ADVICE FROM A PROFESSIONAL FREQUENT FLYER

Tracy Christoph has been a flight attendant for twenty years—eight of which have been with JetBlue Airways, where she's currently a Boston-based in-flight crewmember. If anyone knows how to fly light and fly right, it's her. Read on for her sage advice.

1. **A twenty-one-inch roll-aboard is essential;** it has lots of pockets inside and out, and fits into any overhead bin on any plane. Trade in your purse for a messenger bag when you travel (I have three 8" x 9" ones: fur, leather, and one that's water-resistant). They're small enough to fit under your seat on the plane and under your coat for safe traveling, and large enough to fit your important documents and money.

2. **Pashminas are the most multi-faceted piece of clothing;** I never fly without mine! It can be used as a scarf or a shawl to match an outfit; for temperature changes if I get cold so I don't have to pack a separate blanket or purchase one; rolled up and used as a pillow; or even spread out for use as a pool or beach blanket.

3. **Comfort is key when flying.** A small pair of stud earrings (comfortable for sleeping on the plane) and a polyester black dress (that doesn't wrinkle!) are versatile outfits that you can dress up or down.

4. **For those nervous fliers out there, I compare flying to driving down a rocky road in my hometown;** it may get a little bumpy sometimes, but it's still safe! People ask me how I'm so relaxed about flying and I tell them that walking around a plane after all these years feels like I'm hanging out in my living room.

AT YOUR DESTINATION

Traveling for business? Hopefully, you've got a coworker along for the ride. Go over each day's itinerary the night before, marking down meeting spots and arranging transportation.

Save any shopping bags you acquire throughout your trip. When you're packing up to go home, use them to store damp swimsuits, dirty clothes, or sandy flip flops.

Always lock your suitcase when you leave it behind in a room. It's not hotel maids we distrust, but fellow travelers that might not be so honest.

Be mindful of what you're eating, but don't go crazy watching your diet. You're on vacay, girl! If you overload on dessert, forgive yourself—and just hit the hotel gym in the a.m.

Before you do anything in your hotel room, do a quick sweep for bed bugs. Eww, we know, but it could ruin everything if you're stuck in a room with them. A quick peek under the mattress and behind the headboard should suffice.

Test out your room safe before you use it. If it doesn't work, call the front desk. And if it does, take a photo of what you're putting in there—so you can make sure nothing was taken out.

When you're shopping for souvenirs, always negotiate on price.

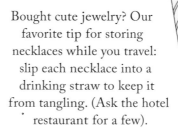

Bought cute jewelry? Our favorite tip for storing necklaces while you travel: slip each necklace into a drinking straw to keep it from tangling. (Ask the hotel restaurant for a few).

Learn something. No matter how drunk you plan on getting, or how much you want to unplug your brain, every travel experience you have should enrich your life somehow—otherwise, it's a complete waste. Take a tour or talk to locals in town, to absorb a little culture. You may learn something about yourself in the process.

Make use of the concierge! They typically know everything and anything about your destination and are there to help. Ask about restaurants, tours, whatever will make your trip more fun and easier for you.

Pack a box of granola bars and a water bottle with a built-in purifier. It doesn't matter what country you're in; when you're off the beaten path and completely starving, you'll be thanking us.

Use a translator app on your phone if you're going somewhere where English isn't their main language. Speaking their native tongue is a sign of respect and will typically get you better treatment wherever you go.

In many tourist laden towns, it's easy to get scammed with beggars on the street or people with a story about "losing their bus pass." Keep a few small bills on you in case you feel like you can't get away. Otherwise, a polite "I'm sorry, I have nothing on me" should do the trick.

Once you're out and about, don't open up a giant map on the sidewalk. You'll scream tourist. Instead, duck into a shop or bathroom if you get lost so you don't look like an easy target.

Real Chick Tip

Do not fly on an empty stomach. Don't assume the airline is going to provide snacks or meals. I have been in tears from hunger before because I did not plan ahead and had hoped the flight would be serving refreshments. It didn't, and I was starving with another four hours to go until I arrived home.

–Kristen, 27, NYC, event planner

GET THE BEST DEAL AROUND

We asked Fulvia Montresor, travel expert at **Hotwire.com** for some insider advice on scoring sweet deals and where. Remember the buzz words in bold: **Bigger hotels** tend to give the best discounts or extras, like dining and spa credits. In general, the more rooms a property has, the harder it will be to fill those rooms, thus the more they will need to discount to entice travelers. **Hotels in big cities** (think Chicago and NYC) discount their prices on the weekends due to a lack of business travel and to lure leisure travelers. **Resorts often offer package promotions,** especially in the off-season when the tourist traffic is down, so don't only consider stand-alone hotels. And **Paris and other larger European cities** are quiet during August because locals tend to flock to beach towns for their summer holiday, so it's cheap and you'll have easier access to activities than at busier times of the year.

MONEY TIPS FOR WHEN YOU'RE ABROAD

From how to save while you're away to being the most financially prepared chica around, we tapped Peggy Goldman, president of Friendly Planet Travel, for advice. Read on:

1. Never exchange money until you arrive at your destination. You will always get a better exchange rate than if you change money in the USA.

2. Use ATMs as you travel to get small amounts of cash for minor purchases. Many cards today have low or no transaction fees and exchange rates are often very good.

3. Let your credit card company know you'll be traveling and where you're going. That's the best way to avoid the embarrassment of an over-protective security policy denying the charge.

4. Check carefully about any entry or departure fees that cannot be prepaid. Even if you think you have paid all taxes, keep some extra cash on hand for your departure. Then, if there is a surprise exit fee, you won't have to pass the collection plate among total strangers.

5. Don't carry a lot of cash or multiple credit cards with you during the day. Take enough cash for small purchases and a credit card with you, preferably in a well-hidden pouch, and leave the rest at your hotel in the safe.

CONCLUSION

There you have it! The beauty of a book is that it's something you can refer to time and time again. The advice you've read isn't lost because you've lost your website bookmarks. It's always ready and willing to shell out solid advice at a moment's notice. We'll leave you with just a few final tips that didn't fit in anywhere else but here.

YOUR TWENTIES DO COME TO AN END.
So don't waste your time regretting mistakes, procrastinating on your career, and fighting with people older than you. Most of the time, they know better.

YOU HAVE TO TURN DOWN INVITATIONS—AND DON'T FEEL BAD ABOUT IT.
The fastest way to get burnt out is to say yes to every. little. thing. White lies to get out of book club, your friend's daughter's birthday party, or even happy hour are totally acceptable and sometimes necessary to get the down and alone time we all need.

UNDERSTAND THE IMPORTANCE OF HONESTY.
Can't make it to that happy hour we just mentioned? Just tell it like it is and say, I just want to sit at home in my pajamas tonight. I'm sorry. Honesty really is the best policy.

YOU SHOULD TALK TO A LOT OF PEOPLE.

Your seatmate on an airplane, the woman behind the table at the farmers market, we mean anyone. You never know what it could lead to—a job opportunity, a blind date, a free dermatology screening. Jeez, who knows?

YOU STILL DON'T KNOW IT ALL.

It's important to admit that we still have a long way to go in life. If you're at a job that is still a lot of grunt work, don't tell yourself you should already be a VP. We've still got a few more decades of learning to do. And besides, when we're the thirty-something VP, we'll probably be passing off some less exciting work on our younger interns. It all comes back around.

BELIEVE IN THE IMPORTANCE OF FRIENDSHIP AND FAMILY.

You will go through many ups and downs in your twenties and the support of true friends will see you through. In fact, you'll realize exactly who your most genuine friends are and by the time you hit thirty, we're guessing you'll have a very strong support system. One "real chick," Jeannine from New York, told us the best tip she can give is to surround yourself with women that already have amazing tips of their own. Now that's something we can get behind.

TAKE YOUR VITAMINS, WEAR SUNBLOCK, DRINK LOTS OF WATER, AND EXERCISE.

Yes, we've said it before. But when you hit twenty-nine, you might start to notice the subtlest changes in your body. A slower metabolism, a sore ankle on the treadmill. Put some good practice into place early on. Trust us. It'll help you in the long run.

With that, we leave you. But we want to hear from you! Send us your tips—or feedback—to tipsfor20s@gmail.com. No robotic responses, just us. And while we didn't save your life, change your religion, or get you married in one book, we do hope we made your twenties a little easier. Those tips, when you go, "Hey, I did *not* know that," are little gems that pack a lot of punch. And it's all about helping a sister out. As a boutique owner in Hoboken once said to us when we graciously accepted a spare hair tie on a particularly hot day, "Hey, ya gotta play for Team Pink, ya know?" Happy twenties!

ACKNOWLEDGMENTS

HOT TIP: ALWAYS THANK ANYONE
AND EVERYONE WHO WAS THERE FOR YOU.

FROM BOTH OF US . . .

We'll start with our agent extraordinaire, Kent D. Wolf of
Lippincott Massie & McQuilkin. He took on two girls with
an idea and ended up with two royal pains who asked a million
questions. Thank you for believing in us! Same goes to our
fabulous editor Kristin Kulsavage (KK!), for being the most
easy-going person we could have ever hoped to work alongside.
To everyone at Skyhorse Publishing who touched our project in
one way or another, you all seriously rock. And to our super-
talented, twentysomething illustrator over in Sweden, Kristina
Hultkrantz: Puss o kram, and thanks for bringing our tips to life
through your gorgeous drawings! Grazie also to Beth Lipton
and Jayna Maleri for their initial support when we first set out
to draft a proposal and pitch to agents.

Meat isn't enjoyable without the potatoes, so thanks to each
and every expert that took the time to engage with us and
thoughtfully put together their very best tips for the readers of
this book. And to all of our "real chicks," the twentysomething
ladies we tapped for contributions—and all the ones who forked
over cash for this book (we approve of your financial decision)
—you're the heart and soul of the project. Thanks for coming
along with us.

FROM LAURA . . .

First and foremost, I must thank my co-author and partner in writing crime Melissa for thinking of me when she first had this idea for a book. It is because of your dedication and enthusiasm that this ever got off the ground. Your belief in the project—and in me—has been a gift. You are such a dear friend to me and there is no one else that I could have done this with. Let's hope this is our first book of many.

I have to acknowledge my best friends who were the inspiration behind many of these tips. A decade of friendship has taught me my most valuable life lessons because of the beautiful women I surround myself with. Lots of love must go to friends from Maine to Manhattan, especially Lombo, Jeannine, Eileen, Nana, Monique, Jacq, Bitzy, and the one and only Amanda. I must also thank two of my mentors, Krissy Tiglias and Laura Fenton, for giving me my first internship and being a support ever since.

To my dearest love Alex, known to many as "my lobsterman." I could fill this entire book with tips on love, mostly because of what you've taught me. Thank you for the endless support, love, and laughs.

A huge thanks goes to my family. I wish I could thank you all individually, but instead, a big mille grazie goes to the Serino's, Fitzgerald's, Sabo's, Sikorski's, Armstrong's, and to the world's most amazing grandparents I could have ever had. Thanks to Sara and Tommy for always cheering on their big sister.

And finally, I owe everything I am to my parents. Love and gratitude must go to my father for teaching me how to write. I suppose I get my humor from you, too, so thanks. And to my mother—your presence as a strong, smart woman in my life made me realize that I wanted to be just like you when I grew up. I live every day hoping I make you both proud.

FROM MELISSA . . .

Without my co-author and very cherished friend, Laura Serino, this book would have been DOA. Her wit, sassy voice, persistence, and creativity gave this book style. I can't imagine having written it with anyone else. Thank you for joining me on this journey and for making it so much fun, and yes, let's please keep going.

My friends! My Shaker girls (Megan, Kristen, Lauren, Hillary, Sara), my Tufts ladies, my Albany besties, my Hoboken loves, my NYC colleagues, my relatives (the Fiorenzas, Haskells, Cannons, and so on), sisters-in-law (Cathy and Lauren!), professors (Michael Blanding!), and more . . . You all know who you are—and you mean the world to me. Thanks for all your life tips, all the time.

To my talented brother and sister, Jeff and Cassie: You guys inspire and impress me every day, and I love you both. Thank you for your encouragement and support.

My husband, Matt Cannon. I had written a lot of first chapters before we started dating, but your endless enthusiasm for my passion got me to keep on writing. I heart you, handsome man.

And finalmente, my brilliant parents—Vittorio and Donna. Pops, thanks for saying "write a book" enough times that I finally sat down and wrote a book. Your encouragement and belief in me drives me in everything I do. Mom (aka the tip-giver to end all tip-givers), because of your intellect, beauty, and strength, I will always keep my head up, and I will always have a goal to strive for: to be just like you and Dad when I grow up.

MEET THE AUTHORS

Melissa Fiorenza
- Left NYC to live the suburban life upstate near Saratoga Springs
- Met her husband in junior high, but began dating 13 years later
- Would rather sweat on the beach than freeze in the cold
- Once had a voicemail from Sinbad (long story)
- Learned Italian curse words at a very young age

Laura Serino
- Moved to an island off the coast of Maine to be with a very handsome lobsterman
- Runs a street style blog that chronicles Maine fashion
- Dreams of owning a 19th-century farm-house with chickens and a goat
- Quotes Oprah Winfrey on a daily basis
- Buys and sells vintage clothes, but secretly wishes she could just sew her own

Kristina Hultkrantz

- Graduated high school twice
- Bought a one way-ticket to Sweden to explore her roots and is still living there five years later
- Has never opened a can of soda or beer, ever